The Ultimate SPAM Cookbook

==

300+ Simple Recipes for Preserving Meat, Pies, Rollers, Snacks and Much More to Enjoy with Your Family and Friends

==

Keven M. Burgin

TABLE OF CONTENTS

INTRODUCTIONS	9
RECIPES	11
SPAM MUSUBI FOR THE HOLIDAYS	11
SHEET PAN DINNER WITH POTATOES AND GREEN	12
DINNER ON A SHEET PAN, FAJITAS CLASSICOS	13
STIR-FRY WITH CLASSIC AND BROCCOLI	14
SPAM YAKITORI	15
SANDWICH WITH TAMAGO	15
RISOTTO WITH SPAM	16
SPAM BURGERS WITH A BBQ GLAZE	17
HO FUN WITH BLACK BEANS	18
SPAM KATSUDON	19
MENUDO DE SPAM (FILIPINO SPAM)	21
CHILAQUILES VERDES WITH SPAM	21
MUSUBI WITH SPAM (CLASSIC MUSUBI)	22
BENEDICT WITH SPAM AND SRIRACHA	23
SPAM SISIG "SPAM SANDWICH"	24
GRILLED SPAM BURGERS WITH HOISIN GLAZE AND QUICK-PICKLED CUCUMBERS	25
SPAM PANINI	26
COBB SALAD WITH SPAM	27
PASTA CARBONARA WITH SPAM	28
RISOTTO CROQUETTES WITH CREAMY SPAM	29
BREAKFAST SANDWICH WITH SPAM, EGG, AND CHEESE	30
SPAM CAKE FOR A BIRTHDAY	31
TACOS CON SPAM CHEESY (CHEESY SPAM PASTOR)	33
SPAM, EGGS, AND RICE	34

2 | Page

- BREAKFAST MUSUBI MADE WITH SPAM AND REAL HORMEL BACON 35
- BREAKFAST SANDWICH WITH SPAM 36
- BREAKFAST BURRITOS WITH SPAM 36
- CALIFORNIA SPAM FRIED RICE 37
- MUSUBI WITH ADOBO SPAM 38
- SPAM SAIMIN 39
- PIZZA WITH SPAM MUSUBI 40
- CRUNCHY ROLL WITH SPAM MUSUBI 41
- HAWAIIAN SKILLET WITH SPAM 42
- GRILLED SPAM CHEESE SANDWICH WITH BRIE AND PEACHES 43
- CRUNCHY NUGGETS MADE WITH SPAM 43
- SPAM CLASSIC MAC & CHEESE IN A SINGLE SKILLET 44
- SPAM CLASSIC KIMBAP 45
- BUDAE JJIGAE ARMY STEW WITH SPAM 46
- MUSUBI WITH SPAM FOR BREAKFAST 47
- BAKED FRENCH TOAST WITH SPAM 48
- SANDWICH WITH SPAM ON A BAGEL 49
- FRIED SPAMBALL SERVED WITH SPICY RANCH DRESSING 50
- SPAM SLIDER WITH A BLOODY MARY FLAVOUR 51
- EGGS WITH SPAM CHEESY TOAST 52
- CORNDOG WITH LONO SPAM 53
- SPAM CLASSIC AND BEEF RAMEN 54
- SANDWICHES WITH SPAM AND CHEESE 55
- TACOS WITH SPAM 55
- SUMMER ROLLS WITH SPAM 56
- CLASSIC BIBIMBAP BOWL WITH SPAM 57
- GYROS WITH SPAM 59
- KABOBS MADE WITH SPAM TERIYAKI, PINEAPPLE, AND RED PEPPERS 60
- TACOS WITH SPAM A LA BARBACOA CON JALAPENOS Y SALSA DE PINEAPPLE ..60

SPAM SLAW WITH NOODLES IN AN ASIAN STYLE	61
MUSUBI WITH TERIYAKI AND TAKUAN SPAM	63
POKE BOWL WITH SPAM	64
CUBAN SPAMWICH, FRESHLY PRESSED IN A HOT PRESS	64
BAKED HASHBROWNS WITH SPAM	65
SPAM WITH SCALLOPED POTATOES	66
BENEDICT, THE SPAM BENEDICT	67
PIZZA ROLLS WITH SPAM	68
SPAM CANTONESE SWEET AND SOUR	70
ICE CREAM WITH MAPLE AND BROWN SUGAR SPAM.	71
CASSEROLE DE PIZZA CON SPAM	72
EGG ROLLS WITH SPAM-YUM FILLING	73
MEATBALLS WITH SPAM FROM THE FAR EAST AS AN APPETIZER	74
VEGGIE SKEWERS WITH SPAM	75
SALAD DE PASTA DE SPAM (WESTERN PASTA SALAD)	76
SPAM SKILLET IN A VARIETY OF COLORS	77
PIZZA WITH SPAM FOR BREAKFAST	78
MINI-QUEUES WITH SPAM AND SPINACH	79
SANDWICH WITH SPAM ON THE BIG ISLAND OF HAWAII	80
SPAM AND SCRAMBLED EGGS	80
SLIDERS WITH KC BBQ SPAM	81
CHEESEBALLS MADE WITH SPAM	82
SPAM BREAKFAST BAKE	83
WAFFLES FILLED WITH SPAM AND CHEESE	84
SLIDERS MADE WITH SPICY SPAM	85
MUSUBI TACOS WITH CAULIFLOWER RICE AND SPAM	86
FRENCH TOAST STICKS WITH SPAM	87
PASTA WITH SPAM	88
BREAKFAST ENCHILADAS WITH SPAM CASSEROLE	89

WHEN PIGS FLY, SPAM BITES	90
WONTONS FILLED WITH SPAM	91
HAWAIIAN PIZZA WITH SPAM	93
CASSEROLE OF TATER TOTS WITH SPAM	93
SPAMALICIOUS FIESTA DIP	94
JACK, SPAM, AND OTHERS	95
SANDWICH WITH SPAM IN THE STYLE OF THE MONTE CRISTO	96
SPAM MONKEY BREAD	96
SPAM LAZY DAY CASSEROLE	98
BITES OF SPAM ENCASED WITH BACON	99
APPETIZER WITH SPAM (ISLAND STYLE)	100
SOUP WITH SPAM AND GNOCCHI	101
MUSUBI WITH BBQ SPAM	102
EAST MEETS WEST IN THE FORM OF SPAM ROLLS	103
JUICY LUCY SPAM BURGER HAMBURGER	104
BREAKFAST MUFFINS WITH SPAMKINS	104
SPAM RED FLANNEL HASH	106
SPAMLT OG SLIDER	106
SPAM POTATO SALAD	107
BABY REDS WITH SPAMENTO CHEESE	108
BBQ SANDWICH WITH SPAM	109
SPAMMY TOTS	110
SPAM	111
SPAM WITH RAMEN NOODLES	115
SPAM WITH RAMEN FROM GENERAL TSO'S KITCHEN	116
NACHOS WITH CREAMY SPAM AND PASTA	116
SPAMMY CAKES	118
RED ONION AND SLAW, SPAM STREET TACOS	119
SPAM PHO	120

CHEESECAKE WITH SPAM AND PINEAPPLE	121
CASSEROLE WITH POTATO PIEROGI WITH SPAM ADDED	123
BURGER WITH SPAM AND RAMEN	124
BISCUITS WITH SPAM, BACON, EGGS, AND CHEESE	124
SANDWICH MADE WITH GRILLED CHEESE AND EGGS AND SPAM	125
MUSUBI BITES WITH ADOBO FRIED RICE AND SPAM	126
SPAMLT	127
SANDWICH WITH SPAM (KATSU)	128
SPAM SALAD WITH A BOW TIE	129
CHOWDER WITH SPAM AND POTATOES	129
SLOPPY JOES WITH SPAMBURGER	130
TURKEY ROLLUPS WITH SPAM	131
SLT FOR THE ULTIMATE SPAM BREAKFAST	131
SPAM HOT CHEESY PARTY DIP	133
TACOS WITH SPAM	133
HAWAII KABOBS WITH SPAM CORDON BLEU	134
BREAKFAST HASH WITH SPAM	135
THAI SALAD CUPS WITH SPAM	136
TURKEY POT PIE WITH SPAM	137
MUSUBIS WITH SPICED CHILLI AND GARLIC	138
SPAM LOCO MOCO	138
MINI SPAM NACHO BURGERS	139
SPAM FRIED TO DELICIOUSNESS!	140
MUSUBI WITH TERIYAKI KATSU AND SPAM	141
SPAMBURGER HAMBURGER	142
SPAM SPUDS	142
BISCUITS WITH JALAPENOS	143
MUSUBI WITH SPAM	144
FRITTATA WITH SPAM	145

PAELLA WITH SPAM	146
SPAM BARS	147
SPAMBURGERTM WITH HAWAIIAN SPAMBURGERTM SAUCE	148
HOT BROWNS WITH SPAM	149
APPLE'S SPAM TURNOVER	150
PINEAPPLE FRIED RICE AND SPAM WITH REDUCED SODIUM	151
NO DELICIOUS SPAM TERIYAKI	152
DIP WITH BACON, SPAM, AND CHEESEBURGER	153
OMELET WITH SPAM (WESTERN OMELET)	154
TACOS CON SPAM (SPAM STREET TACOS)	155
CORNED BEEF AND CABBAGE PANCAKES	156
SLIDERS WITH SPAM AND SAUCY MEATBALLS	156
ENCHILADAS WITH SPAM	157
SPAM EGG SALAD SANDWICH SPREAD	159
SPAM CRACKLES ON THE ISLANDS OF OAHU	159
RICE BITES WITH SPICY SPAM	161
DONUTS FILLED WITH SPAM	161
SPAM SANDWICH ON A PHILLY-DILLY ROLL	162
CAULIFLOWER GRATIN WITH SPAM	164
QUESADILLAS WITH SPAM	165
BREAKFAST MUFFINWICH WITH SPAM	166
SPAM AND NOODLES	166
SPAM CARBONARA	167
PRETZEL NUGGETS WITH HICKORY SMOKED SPAM	168
PIGGIES ON A BLANKET MADE WITH HAWAIIAN SPAM	170
REUBEN'S SPAM ROLL-UPS	171
HASH WITH SPAM, PUMPKIN SPICE, AND FALL VEGETABLES	171
GRILLED CHEESE WITH SPAM, PUMPKIN SPICE, AND CHEDDAR	172
BREAD PUDDING WITH HAWAIIAN SPAM	173

ORIGINAL BAKED SPAM 174

BURRITO MUSUBI 175

MUSUBI WITH KIMCHI FRIED RICE 176

LONO AMERICAN MUSUBI 177

HAWAIIAN LOCAL BURGER 178

BAKED BEANS 179

HUEVOS CHILAQUILES (CHILAQUILES EGGS) 180

MACARONI AND CHEESE BAKE 181

BACON SPAM AND POTATO PANCAKES 182

BURGERS WITH SPAM 182

CUPCAKES WITH SPAM-A-LICIOUS FROSTING AND SALTED CARAMEL GLAZE..183

SPAM SANDWICHES ON THE BARBECUE 184

SPAM AND BACON, MAKING DEVILED EGGS 185

SPAM MUSUBI 186

SPAM FRIED RICE 187

TACOS DE SPAM 188

TACOS WITH SPAM SHREDDED 189

SANDWICHES WITH HAM AND CHEESE (PA-SPAM-MI) 190

SPAM-OCADO HASH 191

THE SPAM ON THE MOVE 191

SPAM AND POTATO SOUP 192

SPAM, RED BEANS, AND RICE 193

SPAM MUSUBI 194

BURGERS MADE WITH SPAM 195

PAD THAI WITH SPAM 195

MINI SPAM SANDWICHES 196

THE END 197

INTRODUCTIONS

WHAT IS SPAM MADE OF?

What distinguishes Spam from other items produced from chopped meats cooked and mashed together (think scrapple): Spam is manufactured entirely of pork shoulder and ham, with no additional hog leftovers.

Pork shoulder is now regarded as a high-quality cut of pork, but it was not in 1937. Pork shoulder is readily available in supermarkets, and many people braise it until it falls apart. Pork shoulder is used to produce sausage because it offers the ideal meat-to-fat ratio for making the most fabulous sausages. When a hog steak is sliced and cooked, it is called shoulder meat.

The second meat is ham, similar to what you'd get in a deli and put in a sandwich.

The remaining ingredients are salt, potato starch to bind the meat together and keep moisture, and pure sugar.

WHAT DOES SPAM STAND FOR?

We enjoy asking this question because there isn't always an answer. Some people believe it refers to a kind of specially processed American meat. Some think it's a combination of "spice" and "ham," but that's weird because the original Spam didn't include any spices. Another myth goes that at a New Year's Eve party, there was a contest to name it, and after a few toasts, someone shouted "Spam!" and the name stayed. We'll let you choose which story you think is the most compelling, and you can stick with it.

THE IMPACT OF WWII AND THE KOREAN WAR ON SPAM

During WWII, the United States purchased 150 million pounds of Spam. It was the only type of meat that could withstand the long boat rides to Hawaii and Guam. While American troops learned to loathe the pork and shared their dislike back home, the custom of eating Spam in Japan and Hawaii took off. Spam was introduced to the country by US service members stationed there during the Korean War, and it is still trendy.

Spam Musubi and Spam Fried Rice are two of the most popular Spam-related recipe search on Google today, thanks to these cultures' Asian roots. You'll notice that we have recipes for both as you scroll down. Spam is available in 14 different flavors if you want to try something new.

WAYS TO ENJOY SPAM

Musubi is rice with Spam wrapped in the nori seaweed used for sushi drizzled with a sweet soy sauce famous in

Hawaii. It can be as simple as that or elevated with sesame seeds, scallions, or teriyaki sauce.

In Japan, a runny egg is a simple topper for a bowl of noodles. Since Spam and eggs are a perfect pair, adding Spam to a noodle bowl is a given.

And just about everywhere, Spam and eggs are a breakfast staple.

RECIPES

SPAM MUSUBI FOR THE HOLIDAYS

INGREDIENTS:
- 1 (12-ounce) can SPAM Classic, sliced into 8 halves
- 1 cup cranberry sauce that was left over
- 4 cups leftover stuffing that has been warmed
- 2 nori sheets, cut into 8 strips each

INSTRUCTIONS:
1. Cook the SPAM Classic slices in a large pan over medium-high heat for 3 to 5 minutes, or until they are browned. Cook for 1 to 2 minutes, basting periodically with cranberry sauce until the cranberry sauce is entirely glazed. Remove the skillet from the heat.
2. Using a musubi press or a plastic-lined SPAM Classic, place 1/3 cup filling on top of a nori strip and press down to compact. To

finish the filling, place a glazed SPAM Classic slice on top of it. Remove the item from the press or can.
3. Wrap each nori sheet in a single layer. To attach the two ends, moisten one end gently with water. Make another eight by repeating the process.

SHEET PAN DINNER WITH POTATOES AND GREEN

INGREDIENTS:
- 12-pound Yukon gold potatoes, diced
- 2 tablespoons olive oil, split
- 1 teaspoon salt, divided
- 1/2 teaspoon pepper, divided
- 1/2-pound green beans, trimmed
- 1 (12-ounce) can SPAM Classic, sliced
- 1/2 cup mayonnaise
- 1/2 cup sour cream
- Two tablespoons of grainy Dijon mustard.
- 1 tbsp. of apple cider vinegar
- 1 tablespoon pure maple syrup
- 2 tablespoons parsley, finely chopped

INSTRUCTIONS:
1. Preheat the oven to 425 degrees Fahrenheit. Potatoes, 1 tablespoon oil, 1/2 teaspoon salt, and 1/4 teaspoon pepper are mixed on a broad-rimmed baking sheet using tongs. Spread out to provide complete coverage.
2. Bake for 30 minutes until the potatoes are tender-crisp but not mushy. Organize the potatoes on one side of the baking sheet. Green beans should be placed on a baking pan. Drizzle the remaining oil over the top—season with the remaining salt and pepper to taste. Bake the SPAM Classic slices on a baking sheet

for 15 minutes. 15 to 20 minutes, turning SPAM Classic slices once during baking, or until veggies are tender and SPAM Classic slices are golden brown, depending on how large your SPAM Classic slices are

3. *Whisk together the mayonnaise, mustard, vinegar, and maple syrup in a small mixing basin. Add in the parsley and mix well. Toss with the sheet pan supper you made earlier.*

DINNER ON A SHEET PAN, FAJITAS CLASSICOS

INGREDIENTS:
- *1 big white onion, peeled and sliced into strips*
- *1 green pepper, peeled and chopped into strips*
- *1 red pepper, peeled and sliced into strips*
- *3 tablespoons extra-virgin olive oil, divided*
- *1 (12-ounce) can SPAM Classic, cut into strips*
- *2 teaspoons taco seasoning mix from a (1.25-ounce) packet, divided*
- *1 (12-ounce) packet of taco seasoning mix*
- *1/4 cup crumbled cotija cheese, to taste*
- *cilantro, finely chopped*
- *slices of lime*
- *flour tortillas in the shape of fajitas*

INSTRUCTIONS:
1. *Preheat the oven to 425 degrees Fahrenheit. Prepare a big baking sheet pan with a rim and arrange the onion and peppers in a single layer. 2 teaspoons of oil should be drizzled on top. One tablespoon of taco seasoning on top of the mixture. 10 minutes of roasting veggies*
2. *One teaspoon of taco spice and 1 tablespoon of taco oil should be drizzled on top before serving. Toss in the SPAM Classic slices*

into the pan. Roast for 8 to 16 minutes, or until veggies are soft and SPAM Classic strips are lightly browned, depending on how large your vegetables are.
3. Garnish with cheese and cilantro if desired. Toss with lime wedges and tortillas before serving.

STIR-FRY WITH CLASSIC AND BROCCOLI

INGREDIENTS:
- 1/2 cup of water
- 1/4 cup soy sauce
- 2 tablespoons brown sugar
- 1 tablespoon grated ginger.
- 1 tablespoon cornstarch
- 1 garlic clove, peeled and minced
- canola oil (split into 2 tablespoons)
- One can (12 ounces) of SPAM is Traditionally prepared and sliced into bite-sized pieces.
- 4 cups broccoli florets (fresh or frozen)
- 1 small onion, thinly sliced (about 1 inch thick)
- rice that has been cooked to a crisp

INSTRUCTIONS:
1. Combine the water, soy sauce, brown sugar, ginger, cornstarch, and garlic in a small mixing bowl.
2. One tablespoon of oil should be heated in a large pan over medium-high heat. Stir-fry the SPAM Classic in the oil for 2 to 3 minutes, or until it begins to brown. Remove the pan from the heat.
3. Continue to cook the broccoli and onion in the same pan, using the remaining 1 tablespoon oil, over medium-high heat for 4 to 5 minutes, or until crisp-tender. Add the soy sauce mixture to the pan and stir well. Cook, constantly stirring, for 1 to 2 minutes, or

until the sauce has thickened. Return the SPAM Classic to the pan and cook until hot. Serve with a side of rice.

SPAM YAKITORI

INGREDIENTS:
- SPAM Classic (12-ounce can) chopped into cubes.
- 4 scallions, thinly sliced into 1-inch pieces
- a third of a cup of yakitori sauce

INSTRUCTIONS:
1. Preheat the grill to a medium setting.
2. Alternatively, in a crosshatch pattern, thread SPAM Classic and scallions onto ten (4-inch) skewer.
3. Turning the skewers regularly and brushing with yakitori sauce will keep the kabobs hot and well-grilled for 8 minutes or until they are hot and well-grilled.

SANDWICH WITH TAMAGO

INGREDIENTS:
- Two slices of SPAM Classic.
- 4 hard-boiled eggs, peeled and diced
- 1 medium-sized soft-boiled egg, peeled and cut lengthwise
- 2 pieces of plain white bread
- 5 tablespoons mayonnaise
- a quarter teaspoon of salt
- a half teaspoon of sugar
- 1/8 teaspoon freshly ground black pepper, finely ground

- 1 tablespoon chives, finely chopped

INSTRUCTIONS:

1. Cook the SPAM Classic slices in a small pan over medium-high heat for 3 to 4 minutes, until they are crispy and browned.
2. Hard-cooked eggs should be cut in half lengthwise. Transfer the yolks to a medium-sized mixing bowl. Using a fork, lightly mash the yolks. Combine the mayonnaise, salt, sugar, and pepper in a mixing bowl.
3. Hard-boiled egg whites should be finely chopped. Combine with the mayonnaise mixture. Stir until everything is well-combined.
4. Place the SPAM pieces on one slice of bread horizontally. Serve with soft-boiled egg halves placed face down on top. Spread the hard-cooked egg mixture on top of the soft-cooked egg mixture and spread it out to cover the whole bread piece. Place the remaining bread piece on top. Remove crusts from the pan. Cut the sandwich in half and then in thirds. Garnish with chives if desired.

RISOTTO WITH SPAM

INGREDIENTS:

- One 12-ounce can of SPAM Classic that has been diced tiny
- 12-cup finely cut onion
- 4 tablespoons butter, split
- 12 cups Arborio rice (or any other kind of rice)
- 1/4 cup grated Parmesan cheese
- 6 cups chicken stock (warm)
- 6 cups chicken broth
- 1 tablespoon finely chopped herbs, such as parsley, chives, or thyme
- 1 tablespoon olive oil

INSTRUCTIONS:

1. One tablespoon of butter should be melted in a large shallow saucepan over medium heat. SPAM Classic should be included. Cook for 3 to 4 minutes, or until the bottom of the pan is gently browned. Remove the SPAM Classic from the pan and set it aside. Melt the remaining 3 tablespoons of butter in a small saucepan. Add in the chopped onion and mix well. Cook for 4 to 5 minutes until the onions are transparent, stirring occasionally. Combine the rice and the onion mixture. Cook for 2 minutes until the rice starts to brown and become somewhat opaque around the edges.
2. Transfer two ladles of hot chicken stock into the pan using a scoop to keep the store heated. Mix the rice and reserve with a wooden spoon until well combined. Cook until the rice absorbs the stock and releases its starch, stirring regularly, for about 15 minutes. Maintain an even heat for sufficient time to allow the rice to cook. Add the stock, a ladle at a time, until the rice is barely soft and the mixture is creamy. Remove the pan from the heat. Combine the cheese, herbs, and SPAM Classic that was set aside.

SPAM BURGERS WITH A BBQ GLAZE

INGREDIENTS:
- 1 (12-ounce) can SPAM Classic (or similar)
- barbecue sauce (about 3 tablespoons)
- 4 hamburger buns that have been divided and toasted
- 4 slices pepper jack cheese, sliced thinly
- Red onion, thinly sliced
- Slices of pickles

INSTRUCTIONS:
1. SPAM Classic should be cut into four pieces.

2. Cook SPAM Classic in a large pan over medium-high heat, rotating once, for 5 to 7 minutes, or until it is browned and fully cooked. Barbeque sauce should be brushed on after grilling. Cook for another 1 minute, or until the sauce is gently coated.
3. Cheese should be placed on top of burgers. Cook for 1 minute or until the cheese is melted, whichever comes first. Stack the burgers on top of the buns and garnish them with slices of red onion and pickles.

HO FUN WITH BLACK BEANS

INGREDIENTS:
- 1/2 (12-ounce) can SPAM
- 3 teaspoons oil, split
- 12 teaspoons oil, divided Sodium-reduced by cutting into tiny dice
- 1 small bunch of Chinese chives or 4 thinly sliced green onions (about)
- 1 tablespoon grated ginger.
- 2 garlic cloves, peeled and chopped
- 1 red Fresno chile, seeded and finely sliced
- 1 red onion, finely chopped
- 1/4 cup finely chopped red Thai bird chile, seeded and chopped
- black bean garlic sauce (about 1 tablespoon)
- Shaoxing wine (about 2 teaspoons)
- 6 shiitake mushrooms, stemmed and sliced (or substitute)
- 1 tablespoon dark soy sauce and 3/4 cup chicken broth
- 1 tablespoon light soy sauce (or sesame oil)
- One tablespoon of cornstarch combined with 1 tablespoon of water is all needed.
- freshly made flat, broad rice noodles (around 1 pound)
- 1/2 cup finely chopped cilantro

INSTRUCTIONS:

1. One teaspoon of oil should be heated in a large pan over medium-high heat. Reduce the sodium content of the SPAM—Cook for 3 to 4 minutes until the cheese is golden brown. Toss in the chives. Cook for 1 minute on high heat. Using a slotted spoon, carefully remove the pan from the heat.
2. Add the remaining 2 tablespoons of oil to the same skillet. Stir-fry the ginger, garlic, Fresno chiles, and bird chiles for 2 minutes, or until the chiles are tender and fragrant. Pour in the black bean garlic sauce and the wine. Mushrooms should be included—Stir-fry for 1 minute, or until the vegetables are tender. Combine the broth, dark soy sauce, and light soy sauce in a mixing bowl. Bring the pot to a simmer. In a separate bowl, whisk together the cornstarch mixture—Cook for 1 minute, or until the sauce has thickened. Add in the noodles and mix well. Cook for another 2 minutes, gently turning, until the sauce is thick and the noodles are heated. Add in the cilantro and mix well.
3. Transfer the mixture to a serving basin. Finish with a layer of SPAM Less Sodium and a chive combination.

SPAM KATSUDON

INGREDIENTS:

Katsudon Sauce

- 1.1/2 tablespoons soy sauce
- 12 tablespoons cooking sherry or soju
- 1 tablespoon brown sugar
- 1 tablespoon baking sherry or soju
- 1/4 teaspoon of salt

Deep-frying oil

- 1/2 cup of all-purpose flour
- 1-1/2 cups Panko bread crumbs
- 12-ounce can SPAM Classic, chopped into 4 pieces
- 2 eggs, beaten
- 2 eggs, split
- 1 teaspoon of olive oil
- 1/4 cup finely chopped onion
- 1/4 cup finely chopped leeks
- Katsudon Sauce 4 cups cooked Japanese rice

INSTRUCTIONS:

1. Combine all of the sauce ingredients in a small microwave-safe bowl. Microwave on HIGH (100 percent) for 30 to 40 seconds, or until the sugar is dissolved and the mixture is cooked.

TO GET RID OF SPAM KATSU

1. Heat the oil in a medium saucepan over medium-high heat until it reaches 360°F. Separately, place the flour, breadcrumbs, and 1 egg in shallow mixing basins. Lightly whisk the egg. Using flour, dredge the SPAM and cheese pieces together. Breadcrumbs should be coated after being dipped in an egg.
2. Fry in hot oil until golden brown on both sides. Remove the slices and put them aside.

KATSUDON IS USED FOR SPAM.

1. Cook the onion and leeks for 2 to 3 minutes, or until they are soft, in a medium pan over medium heat until the oil is hot. Serve with sliced SPAM katsu on top.
2. The remaining egg should be beaten. Pour the sauce over the sliced SPAM katsu. Katsudon sauce should be poured over the sliced SPAM katsu. Cover and heat for 30 to 45 seconds until the egg is thoroughly cooked.
3. Serve over a bed of rice.

MENUDO DE SPAM (FILIPINO SPAM)

INGREDIENTS:
- 1 (12-ounce) can SPAM Lite (diced) if desired
- 1 tablespoon of extra-virgin olive oil
- 1 garlic clove, minced
- 1 small onion, diced
- 1 tablespoon olive oil
- 1 medium-sized potato, peeled and chopped
- peel and dice 1 small carrot (about 1 cup)
- 1 can tomato paste (about 6 ounces)
- 1/2 cup beef broth
- 1/3 cup cranberries
- defrosted frozen peas (about 1/3 cup)
- 1 bay leaf
- season with salt and pepper to taste
- a pinch of sugar-cooked white rice to be used as a side dish

INSTRUCTIONS:
1. Cook the diced SPAM Lite in the oil for 3 to 4 minutes, or until it is gently browned, in a large pan over medium-high heat. Garlic and onion should be added at this point—Cook for 2 to 3 minutes, or until the onion is soft.
2. Cook for 2 to 3 minutes after adding the potatoes and carrots. Cook for 1 minute after adding tomato paste. Combine the beef broth, raisins, peas, and bay leaf in a large mixing bowl. Reduce heat to low and cook for 5 to 6 minutes until veggies are tender.
3. Season with salt and pepper to your liking. Add a sprinkle of sugar and mix well. Serve over a bed of white rice that has been cooked.

CHILAQUILES VERDES WITH SPAM

INGREDIENTS:
- SPAM Classic, cut into 1/2-inch cubes from a 12-ounce can
- 2 cups tortilla corn chips (or similar)
- 1 cup green salsa
- 1/2 cup shredded Mexican mix cheese, finely chopped
- Two eggs, fried or scrambled.
- If preferred, garnish with sour cream and cilantro.

INSTRUCTIONS:
1. Preheat the oven to 350 degrees Fahrenheit.
2. Cook SPAM Classic in a pan over high heat for 7 to 9 minutes, or until it is fully browned and crispy. Make a mental note to put it away.
3. Using a large mixing basin, carefully combine tortilla chips and salsa verde until the chips are evenly distributed.
4. Half of the coated chips, half of the SPAM Classic cubes, and half of the cheese are placed in an 8 × 8-inch baking dish and baked until the chips are crispy. Layers should be repeated. Bake for 8 to 10 minutes until the potatoes are cooked, and the cheese has melted.
5. Eggs are placed on top of the chilaquiles. If preferred, garnish with sour cream and cilantro before serving.

MUSUBI WITH SPAM (CLASSIC MUSUBI)

INGREDIENTS:
- 2 tbsp soy sauce
- 1 cup sugar (or 2 teaspoons)
- 1 (12-ounce) can SPAM Classic, sliced into 8 halves
- If desired, add 2 tablespoons of furikake to the dish.
- 3 cups sushi rice that has been cooked

- cut 3 pieces of nori sheets into thirds

INSTRUCTIONS:

1. Soy sauce and sugar should be combined in a small bowl.
2. Cook the SPAM Classic slices in a large pan over medium-high heat for 3 to 5 minutes, or until they are browned. Cook for 1 to 2 minutes until the pieces are coated with the soy sauce sugar mixture. Remove the pan from the heat.
3. Place 1/3 cup rice in a musubi press, or a plastic-lined SPAM classic can on top of a nori strip and press down to compact the rice mixture. Take away the press. Furikake may be sprinkled on top of the rice if desired. Finish with a piece of SPAM Classic. Nori is used for wrapping sushi. The leftover nori strip may be saved for future use. To attach the two ends, moisten one end gently with water. Repeat the process with the remaining components.

BENEDICT WITH SPAM AND SRIRACHA

INGREDIENTS:

- 4 egg yolks
- 3.1/2 teaspoons freshly squeezed lemon juice
- 1 tablespoon water
- 1 cup melted butter
- 1 cup sour cream
- 1 tablespoon sriracha sauce (to taste)
- 1 teaspoon salt
- 1 teaspoon white vinegar
- 8 big quail eggs
- 1 can (12 ounces) of SPAM Cut into 8 pieces
- 4 English muffins that have been divided and lightly toasted
- 1 avocado, thinly sliced, 8 tomato slices
- If desired, garnish with finely chopped fresh cilantro.
- If desired, add red pepper flakes.

INSTRUCTIONS:

1. To create Hollandaise sauce, fill the bottom of a double boiler halfway with water, ensuring the water does not come into direct contact with the top pan. Bring the water to a gentle simmer.
2. In the top of a double-boiler, whisk together the egg yolks, lemon juice, and 1 tablespoon of water until well combined and smooth.
3. Whisk continually as you add the butter to the egg yolk mixture, about 1 or 2 tablespoons at a time. If the sauce gets too thick, add 1 to 2 tablespoons of hot water until it thins out. Whisk until all of the butter has been integrated.
4. Remove from heat and cover with a lid while whisking in the salt and Sriracha.
5. To poach eggs, fill a big pot halfway with water and bring it to a boil.
6. Bring the water to a slow boil and stir in the vinegar.
7. To cook the eggs, carefully break them into boiling water and cook for 2.1/2 to 3 minutes, or until the whites are set, but the yolks are still soft in the middle. Remove the eggs using a slotted spoon and place them on a heated dish.
8. Cook the SPAM Classic in a medium pan over medium-high heat for 3 to 4 minutes, or until it is gently crisped.
9. Cut-side-up English muffins should be placed on serving platters.
10. Distribute the avocado, tomato, SPAM Classic, and poached egg equally on the salad. Hollandaise sauce should be drizzled on top. Depending on your preference, garnish with cilantro and red pepper flakes. Serve as soon as possible.

SPAM SISIG "SPAM SANDWICH"

INGREDIENTS:

- 1 tablespoon of extra-virgin olive oil
- 1 can (12 ounces) of SPAM Cubed versions of classics

- *3 cloves minced garlic*
- *1 medium-sized onion*
- *1 cup calamansi or Key lime juice*
- *1 medium-sized onion, diced*
- *1 medium-sized onion, chopped*
- *1 sliced green chile,*
- *1 sliced red chili,*
- *1 sliced jalapeno*
- *season with salt and pepper to taste*
- *If desired, fried eggs may be added.*
- *Garlic Fried Rice*
- *2 tbsp. vegetable oil*
- *garlic, minced (about 2 teaspoons)*
- *3 cups of cooked rice*
- *1 teaspoon of seasoning salt*

INSTRUCTIONS:

1. *Heat the oil in a large pan over medium-high heat until shimmering. Combine the diced SPAM Classic, onions, and garlic in a large mixing bowl. 10 to 15 minutes, or until SPAM Classic is crisped and veggies are soft, depending on your preference.*
2. *Combine the juice, green chilies, and red chilies in a mixing bowl (if using)—season with salt and pepper to your liking.*
3. *Prepare a sizzling dish by heating it.*
4. *Place the SPAM Classic mixture on a serving plate. Eggs are placed on top. Serve with Garlic Fried Rice as a side dish.*
5. *Heat the oil in a large skillet over medium-high heat until shimmering. Add the garlic and cook for 1 to 2 minutes until it is light brown. Combine the rice and salt in a large mixing bowl— Stir-fry for 2 to 3 minutes, until everything is well blended and cooked.*

GRILLED SPAM BURGERS WITH HOISIN GLAZE AND QUICK-PICKLED CUCUMBERS

INGREDIENTS:

- 1/2 cup of water
- rice vinegar (about a third of a cup)
- 2 tbsp. (tablespoons) sugar
- 1 garlic clove, peeled and minced
- 1 teaspoon grated ginger
- 1/4 teaspoon freshly ground red pepper
- 1 English cucumber, thinly sliced (medium size)
- 1 can (12 ounces) of SPAM Classic
- 3 tablespoons hoisin sauce
- 4 hamburger buns that have been divided and toasted
- Fresh cilantro leaves are used in the preparation of the dish.

INSTRUCTIONS:

1. Add the water, vinegar, sugar, garlic, ginger, and crushed red pepper to a small saucepan. Bring to a boil, stirring constantly. Bring to a boil, then turn off the heat. Cucumber slices should be added. Allow 30 minutes for cooling and resting.
2. SPAM Classic should be cut into four pieces.
3. Cook the SPAM Classic in a large pan over medium-high heat, flipping once, for 5 to 7 minutes, or until it is well cooked. Hoisin sauce should be brushed on top. Cook for another 1 minute, or until the sauce is gently coated. Stack the burgers on top of the buns and garnish with pickled cucumbers and cilantro.

SPAM PANINI

INGREDIENTS:

- SPAM Less Sodium, one 12-ounce can (cut into eight pieces).
- 8 slices of Italian-style bread with 2 teaspoons of extra virgin olive oil

- Italian dressing (around 2 tablespoons)
- 2 tablespoons mayonnaise
- Provolone cheese (eight slices)
- Tomatoes cut into 8 pieces
- 1/2 cup roasted red bell pepper strips (cut into strips)
- 1/2 cup sliced pepperoncini

INSTRUCTIONS:

1. Cook the Spam Less Sodium slices for 3 to 5 minutes, or until they are browned, in a large pan over medium-high heat.
2. Preheat a panini machine or a stovetop panini grill according to the manufacturer's instructions until warm.
3. Oil should be applied to one side of the bread pieces. Place the bread on the work surface with the oil side up.
4. Italian dressing and mayonnaise should be combined in a small bowl. Spread the mixture on the bread pieces on the work surface.
5. One piece of cheese should be placed on top of each bread slice. 2 slices SPAM Less Sodium should be placed on one side of each sandwich. 2 slices tomato, 2 tablespoons roasted red bell pepper strips, and 2 tablespoons pepperoncini should be placed on the opposite side of each sandwich for the final touch.
6. Assemble the four sandwiches by pressing them together.
7. Sandwiches should be grilled in a panini machine for 5-7 minutes, or until the bread is toasted and the cheese is melted.

COBB SALAD WITH SPAM

INGREDIENTS:

- 4 cups of mixed spring greens for babies
- 1 cup grape tomatoes
- 4 cooked eggs (hard-boiled)

- *2 avocados, pitted and finely minced*
- *1 English cucumber, peeled and diced*
- *4 ounces of crumbled blue cheese*
- *1 can (12 ounces) of SPAM Diced and cooked in the traditional manner*
- *2 fluid ounces of Ranch Dressing made with buttermilk*

INSTRUCTIONS:

1. Place the ingredients on a serving plate and mix well. The dressing should be served on the side.

PASTA CARBONARA WITH SPAM

INGREDIENTS:

- *1 tablespoon kosher salt*
- *pasta (about 12 ounces)*
- *4 big quail eggs*
- *1/2 cup parmesan cheese, grated*
- *1/2 cup grated Pecorino Romano*
- *1 can (12 ounces) of SPAM Sodium-reduced, diced*
- *pepper and salt to taste freshly cracked black pepper and sea salt*
- *If preferred, garnish with finely chopped Italian parsley.*

INSTRUCTIONS:

2. Bring 6 quarts of water and 1 tablespoon of salt to a boil. Cook the spaghetti according to the instructions on the box. Drain the pasta, reserving 3/4 cup of the cooking water.
3. Whisk together the eggs and cheeses in a medium-sized mixing basin until well incorporated.
4. Using a large skillet, cook the ingredients over medium-high heat. Cook for 3 to 4 minutes, or until the SPAM Less Sodium is

crispy and brown, before adding the SPAM. Stirring and shaking the pan will help to mix the spaghetti.
5. Turn off the heat and set the pan aside. Immediately add the egg mixture and whisk vigorously until the eggs thicken. If the sauce seems excessively thick, thin it up a little at a time with the pasta water that has been saved.
6. Season generously with freshly cracked black pepper before serving. Dish the spaghetti into individual serving dishes and top with parsley, if preferred. Serve as soon as possible.

RISOTTO CROQUETTES WITH CREAMY SPAM

INGREDIENTS:
- 4 tablespoons of melted butter
- 12-ounce can SPAM Classic, diced small;
- 2 yellow onions, chopped;
- 1-cup Arborio rice;
- 4-cups heated chicken stock;
- 1/4 cup grated Parmesan;
- 1/2 (12-ounce) can SPAM Classic, diced small;
- 1 cup of all-purpose flour
- Two eggs, lightly beaten, equal to 2 cups Panko breadcrumbs are a kind of breadcrumb.
- 4 quarts of canola oil
- If preferred, season with flaky sea salt and your favorite dipping sauce.

INSTRUCTIONS:
1. Melt the butter in a large, shallow saucepan set over medium heat. SPAM Classic should be included. Cook for 3 to 4 minutes, or until the bottom of the pan is gently browned. Add in the chopped onions and mix well. Cook for 4 to 5 minutes until the

onions are transparent, stirring occasionally. Combine the rice, onion, and SPAM Classic in a large mixing bowl. Cook for 2 minutes until the rice starts to brown and become somewhat opaque around the edges.

2. Transfer two ladles of hot chicken stock to the pan using a spoon and set aside. Mix the rice and reserve with a wooden spoon until well combined. Cook, constantly stirring, until the rice begins to soak up the liquid and releases its starch, about 15 minutes. Maintain an even heat for sufficient time to allow the rice to cook. The stock should be added in small amounts until the rice is barely soft and the mixture has reached a smooth consistency. Remove the pan from the heat. Add in the cheese and mix well. Using a shallow baking pan, spread the mixture out. Refrigerate for 1 hour after covering with plastic wrap.

3. Roll the rice mixture into balls that are approximately 1.1/4 cup in size. Separately combine the flour, eggs, and breadcrumbs in a large mixing basin. Toss the rice ball in the flour, shaking off any extra. Dip the rice ball into the beaten eggs and set it aside until the flour absorbs the egg and the rice ball is completely covered in the egg. In the end, roll the rice ball in breadcrumbs. Repeat the process with the remaining rice balls.

4. Heat the oil in a 4-quart saucepan over medium-high heat until it reaches 350°F. Reduce the heat to medium and carefully drop four rice balls into the hot oil to brown. Cook for 3 to 4 minutes until the cheese is golden brown. Remove the rice balls from the pan using a slotted spoon and lay them on a wire rack. Repeat the process with the remaining rice balls. If desired, garnish with flaky sea salt and a dipping sauce if using.

BREAKFAST SANDWICH WITH SPAM, EGG, AND CHEESE

INGREDIENTS:

- In two slices (each measuring 1/4-inch thick), SPAM Sodium intake is reduced.
- 4 Hawaiian dinner rolls (not divided) –
- 2 scrambled eggs
- the equivalent of 2 tablespoons Recipe for Roasted Kimchi Mayo is provided below.
- cheese shredded cheddar (about 1/4 cup)
- 2 teaspoons of melted butter
- Roasted Kimchi Mayo is a condiment made from roasted Kimchi.
- Kewpie Mayo (four tablespoons)
- 2 teaspoons roasted Kimchi, finely minced

INSTRUCTIONS:

1. Preheat the oven to 400 degrees Fahrenheit. Prepare a medium skillet by lightly frying it in oil. Cook the Spam Less Sodium slices until they are light golden brown over medium heat. Remove the pan from the heat. Dinner roll toasted in SPAM (low sodium, low fat).
2. Put together the sandwich with eggs, SPAM, fewer Sodium pieces, cheese, and roasted kimchi mayo to make it a breakfast sandwich.
3. Place in the oven for 2 to 3 minutes to allow the cheese to melt.

SPAM CAKE FOR A BIRTHDAY

INGREDIENTS:
- One can (12 ounces) of SPAM is Sliced into 12 pieces with less sodium.
- 1/2 cup shoyu (soy sauce)
- 1 cup sugar (or 2 teaspoons)
- 4 cups warm, cooked short-grain rice Chicken Fat Miso Paste (recipe follows)
- 4 cups cooked short-grain rice

- 4 tablespoons mirin or rice vinegar, if preferred;
- 3 teaspoons oil, divided;
- 6 eggs, beaten;
- 6 tablespoons water, split
- Furikake (about a third of a cup)
- If desired, sprinkle with finely shredded seaweed.
- Miso Paste made from chicken fat
- a quarter cup of schmaltz (rendered chicken fat)
- 1/4 cup miso (white miso)
- 1 tablespoon of table sugar
- 1 tablespoon grated ginger, minced

INSTRUCTIONS:

1. In a food processor, pulse together all of the chicken fat Miso Paste Ingredients until they are entirely smooth.
2. Preheat the oven to 275 degrees Fahrenheit. Prepare a baking sheet with a rim by lining it with parchment paper. Slices of SPAM with less sodium should be placed in a shallow dish. In a small container, mix the shoyu and sugar; pour over the pieces of SPAM Less Sodium. Marinate for a total of 10 minutes. Place on a baking sheet that has been prepared—Bake for 5 to 6 minutes, or until the mixture is well heated.
3. Prepare a 9-inch springform pan by lining it with aluminum foil or plastic wrap and setting it aside.
4. In a large mixing bowl, combine the Chicken Fat Miso Paste with the mirin or rice vinegar, if preferred, and the rice, seasoning it to taste.
5. One teaspoon of oil should be heated in a medium nonstick pan over medium heat. Fry 2 eggs to make an open-faced omelet that is about the same diameter as the springform pan that has been prepped. Repeat the process with the remaining oil and eggs to make three-egg layers.
6. Place 1 egg omelet in the bottom of the pan that has been prepared. Place a quarter of the rice mixture on top of the egg layer, pushing down with damp palms to produce an equal layer. Furikake should be sprinkled on top of the rice. Add another egg omelet on top, followed by another 14% of the rice mixture,

pushing down to ensure uniform distribution. Furikake may be added on top if desired. 12 SPAM Fewer Sodium slices should be placed on the seasoned rice. Stack another 14 cups of rice on top, pushing down firmly. The final egg omelet, rice, and furikake are placed on top.

7. Allowing the edges of the pan to release, take down the foil or plastic wrap to prepare for serving. Decorative seaweed may be used to finish the dish if desired. The cake should be sliced into pieces using a damp knife.

TACOS CON SPAM CHEESY (CHEESY SPAM PASTOR)

INGREDIENTS:
- 1 (8-ounce) can of pineapple chunks in pineapple juice
- 2 lemons, freshly squeezed (about 4 tablespoons)
- Mexican blend seasoning (about 2 teaspoons)
- 1 tablespoon of table sugar
- 1 can (12 ounces) of SPAM Cut into 18 sticks
- 2 tablespoons vegetable oil, divided
- 2 tablespoons finely chopped white onion
- 1/2 cup finely chopped cilantro, if desired
- 6 ounces queso fresco cheese (fresh cheese)
- 10 corn tortillas.
- 2 limes, peeled and sliced into wedges

INSTRUCTIONS:
1. Pour the ingredients into a large mixing bowl and whisk until well combined (including the pineapple juice). Add the SPAM Classic and let it marinate for ten minutes.
2. Cook for 2 minutes on high heat in a big skillet. Reduce the heat to medium-high and add 1/4 cup of oil to the pan—heat for ten seconds. Toss the SPAM Classic and marinade into the pan with

care. Cook for 5 to 6 minutes, or until the meat is deep golden brown, stirring regularly. Remove the skillet from the heat and put it aside.
3. In a small dish, combine the onion and cilantro and set aside.
4. Heat a large skillet over medium-high heat for 1.1/2 minutes or until hot. A circle more diminutive than a corn tortilla should be formed by placing 1 teaspoon of oil and 2 to 3 tablespoons of cheese on top. Cook for 30 seconds after setting the tortilla over the cheese. Cook for another 10 seconds after carefully turning the cheese and tortilla over. Remove the skillet from the heat. Toss the remaining oil, cheese, and tortillas together and set aside.
5. Sprinkle the SPAM mixture, onion, and cilantro on top of each tortilla. Serve with lime wedges on the side. This makes a total of 10.

SPAM, EGGS, AND RICE

INGREDIENTS:
- 1 can (12 ounces) of SPAM 8 eggs, scrambled,
- 2 cups cooked rice,
- 1/4 cup chopped green onions,
- less sodium, sliced

INSTRUCTIONS:
1. Cook the Spam Less Sodium slices for 3 to 5 minutes, or until they are browned, in a large pan over medium-high heat.
2. Serve with scrambled eggs and rice for a complete meal. Garnish with green onions, if desired.

BREAKFAST MUSUBI MADE WITH SPAM AND REAL HORMEL BACON

INGREDIENTS:
- 1 (12-ounce) can SPAM with REAL HORMEL. a pound of bacon, sliced into 8 slices
- 4 quail eggs
- 2 tbsp mirin
- 1 tbsp. table sugar
- Salt
- the equivalent of two tablespoons of DASH
- 2 teaspoons of extra-virgin olive oil
- 2 nori sheets, cut into 8 strips each
- Furikake (sushi rice): 3 cups cooked sushi rice
- 4 slices of cheddar cheese, halved or quartered

INSTRUCTIONS:
1. Cook SPAM with Real HORMEL Bacon slices in a big pan over medium-high heat for 3 to 5 minutes, or until the SPAM is browned.
2. In a medium-sized mixing bowl, combine the eggs, mirin, sugar, a sprinkle of salt, and the dashi. Oil should be heated in a large nonstick skillet over medium heat. Pour about one-third of the egg mixture into the pan. Once the eggs have begun to firm, fold them in half like an omelet, turning them to the side of the pan to make way for another one-third of the egg mixture. Allow that time to set before rolling the omelet in another way to stack it together. Repeat the process with the remaining egg mixture to form a single-layered rolled omelet. Using an 8-section cutter, cut the cake into 8 parts.
3. Place 1/3 cup rice on top of the nori strip in a musubi press or a SPAM product coated with plastic wrap, then press down to compact the rice. Take away the press. Furikake should be sprinkled on top of the rice. Finish with a split cheese slice and a

bit of the egg. One piece of SPAM with Real HORMEL Bacon should be placed on top. Wrap the nori around the musubi, moistening the edge of the nori to help it stick together. Make another eight by repeating the process.

BREAKFAST SANDWICH WITH SPAM

INGREDIENTS:
- 2 slices each of 1 (12-ounce) can of SPAM Classic
- 4 oz. shredded cheddar cheese
- 2 teaspoons hot sauce (Sriracha)
- 4 tbsp. mayonnaise
- Burger buns (four) that have been gently toasted in the toaster oven
- 2 thinly sliced yellow onions, caramelized in a skillet
- 4 eggs, fried until the desired doneness is achieved

INSTRUCTIONS:
1. Cook the SPAM Classic in a large pan over medium-high heat for 3 to 5 minutes, or until it is browned. Cheese should be placed on top of each SPAM Classic slice.
2. Combine Sriracha and mayonnaise in a small mixing bowl. Spread the mixture on the buns that have been made. Fill each sandwich with one slice of SPAM Classic topped with cheese, caramelized onions, and eggs, and serve immediately.

BREAKFAST BURRITOS WITH SPAM

INGREDIENTS:

- 1 (12-ounce) can SPAM Classic (cut into cubes), drained and rinsed
- 4 big burrito-sized tortillas (about)
- scrambled eggs for four people
- 2 hash brown patties that have been made according to package Instructions
- cheese (about 1 cup shredded cheddar)
- 1-1/2 cups Monterey Jack cheese, shredded
- peeled and pitted avocado (cut into slices)
- 1 cup drained and cooked black beans
- Pico de Gallo (half a cup)

INSTRUCTIONS:
1. Cook the SPAM Classic in a large pan over medium-high heat for 3 to 5 minutes, or until it is browned. Remove the skillet from the heat.
2. Fill each tortilla with the contents in an equal layer. Burritos should be rolled up. Place burritos in a large pan over medium heat and cook for 1 to 2 minutes, rotating once or twice to griddle all sides, until toasted and lightly golden.

CALIFORNIA SPAM FRIED RICE

INGREDIENTS:
- 2 tbsp. extra-virgin olive oil
- 1 small onion, coarsely chopped (about)
- 2 garlic cloves, peeled and minced
- 1 can (12 ounces) of SPAM Cut into cubes; this is a classic.
- Green beans, chopped into 1/4-inch pieces, 2 cups
- 4 cups cooked refrigerated rice
- scrambled eggs (three eggs total)
- 1/4 cup soy sauce
- 1 pinch of table salt

INSTRUCTIONS:

1. Heat the oil in a wok or large frying pan over high heat until shimmering. Add the onion and simmer for 3 to 4 minutes until it becomes translucent. Stir in the garlic for a further 30 seconds— Cook for 3 minutes after adding SPAM Classic.
2. Add the beans to the pan and stir-fry for 3 to 4 minutes, or until they are soft. Cook, constantly stirring, for 3 to 4 minutes more, or until the rice is well heated. Combine the eggs, soy sauce, and salt in a large mixing bowl. Serve as soon as possible.

MUSUBI WITH ADOBO SPAM

INGREDIENTS:
- 2 slices each of 1 (12-ounce) can of SPAM Classic
- a quarter cup of apple cider vinegar
- Mirin or rice vinegar (about 1/4 cup)
- a quarter cup of water
- 2 garlic cloves, peeled and chopped
- Cut 2 green onion whites in half lengthwise and set aside.
- 2 bay leaves, broken into pieces
- 2 tablespoons black peppercorns, finely ground
- 2 teaspoons extra-virgin olive oil
- 3 cups sushi rice that has been cooked
- 4 nori sheets, each half-sheeted

INSTRUCTIONS:

1. Slices of SPAM Classic should be placed in a medium-sized mixing basin. Combine the cider vinegar, mirin, water, garlic, onion, bay leaves, and peppercorns in a large mixing bowl. Allow for a one-hour marinating period.

2. Remove the marinated SPAM Classic slices from the marinade. Keep the marinade aside.
3. Heat the oil in a large skillet over medium-high heat until shimmering. Cook the SPAM Classic Classic for 2 to 3 minutes, or until it is browned on the outside. Add the marinade to the pan and the SPAM Classic slices and cook for 3 to 4 minutes, or until the sauce is mildly sticky.
4. Insert nori sheet halves into the center of the musubi press or plastic-lined SPAM Classic can and press down. Repeat with remaining rice until all of the nori sheet halves are used. Finish with a piece of SPAM Classic. Take away the press.
5. Wrap each nori sheet in a single layer. To attach the two ends, moisten one end gently with water. Make another eight by repeating the process.

SPAM SAIMIN

INGREDIENTS:
- 1 can (12 ounces) of SPAM
- 1-pound fresh saimin or ramen noodles, boiled and drained 4 cups dashi (Japanese soup stock), hot
- 4 ounces kamaboko (fish cake), thinly sliced
- 2 cups fresh spinach, finely chopped
- 4 green onions, finely chopped
  - cup of crispy onion flakes,
- 2 soft-cooked eggs,
- halved jalapeño pepper, thinly sliced
- 4 shiitake mushrooms,
- 1/2 cup soft-cooked eggs

INSTRUCTIONS:
2. Cook the Spam Less Sodium slices for 3 to 5 minutes, or until they are browned, in a large pan over medium-high heat. Using four

soup dishes, divide the noodles evenly. Toss the noodles in the dashi.
3. Divide the SPAM into Fewer Sodium slices and the other ingredients among the bowls in an even layer.

PIZZA WITH SPAM MUSUBI

INGREDIENTS:
- One 12-ounce can of SPAM Classic, cut into eight slices
- a cup of sushi rice that has been cooked with eight sheets of nori
- Toppings suggested include Browned SPAM Classic rounds, furikake, and teriyaki sauce, browned SPAM Classic pieces, chopped Kimchi, green onions, and togarashi browned SPAM Classic rounds, furikake, and teriyaki sauce.

INSTRUCTIONS:
1. To make the rounds, cut two slices of SPAM Classic using a 1.1/2-inch cookie cutter. 2 pieces of SPAM Classic are diced.
2. Cook SPAM Classic slices, rounds, and diced pieces in a big pan over medium-high heat for 3 to 5 minutes, or until thoroughly browned. Remove the skillet from the heat. Each slice should be cut into four strips.
3. Layer 1 nori over 1 layer of rice, leaving a 1-inch border around the top. 4 stips of SPAM Classic should be placed directly below the center of the rice. From the "pizza crust" by rolling it up like a sushi roll.
4. One nori sheet should be cut into a triangular shape to serve as the basis of the pizza slice. Place the sushi roll crust on top of the triangle on a serving platter and serve immediately. A thin coating of rice should be spread across the triangle. SPAM Classic rounds and chopped pieces, as well as the specified toppings, should be placed on top of the pizza slice. Repeat the process to produce four slices.

CRUNCHY ROLL WITH SPAM MUSUBI

INGREDIENTS:
- 2 tbsp soy sauce
- 1 cup sugar (or 2 teaspoons)
- 1 can (12 ounces) of SPAM Classic cut into 8 equal-sized pieces
- 3 cups sushi rice (blanched and cooked)
- 4 nori sheets, sliced in half; 2 eggs, lightly beaten
- 2 cups panko bread crumbs
- Vegetable oil is a kind of oil that comes from plants.
- 3/4 cup unagi sushi sauce
- sesame seeds (about 2 tablespoons)
- 1 cup crumbled shrimp chips
- 1/4 cup green onion, finely chopped

INSTRUCTIONS:
1. Soy sauce and sugar should be combined in a small bowl.
2. Cook the SPAM Classic slices in a large pan over medium-high heat for 3 to 5 minutes, or until they are browned. Cook for 1 to 2 minutes until the pieces are coated with the soy sauce sugar mixture. Remove the skillet from the heat.
3. Place 1/3 cup rice into a musubi press or a SPAM can coated with plastic wrap and press down firmly. Remove from the press and place on top of a nori sheet that has been halved. Wrap the nori around the musubi, moistening the edge of the nori to help it stick together. Make another eight by repeating the process.
4. Place the eggs and breadcrumbs on two shallow plates and set them aside. Each musubi is dipped and rolled in egg, then in panko.
5. 1-inch vegetable oil should be heated in a large pan over medium-high heat. Fry the musubi in the oil, flipping once or twice, for 3 to 5 minutes, or until golden brown on both sides.

6. Using a sharp knife, cut each musubi into four slices. Place 8 pieces on each of the four serving platters. Drizzle each with sriracha mayonnaise and top with Unagi, sesame seeds, shrimp chips, and green onions, if desired.

HAWAIIAN SKILLET WITH SPAM

INGREDIENTS:
- 12-ounce can of SPAM with chopped real Hormel Bacon
- 1 cup pineapple chunks (chopped)
- 1 cup mango chunks (diced)
- a half teaspoon of cumin
- 1/2 teaspoon smoked paprika.
- a half teaspoon of salt
- a half teaspoon of salt with garlic
- Balsamic glaze over hot cooked rice

INSTRUCTIONS:
1. Cook SPAM with bacon, pineapple, mango, cumin, smoked paprika, salt, and garlic powder in a big pan over medium-high heat until the bacon is crispy. Cook for 6 to 8 minutes until the top is beautifully browned.
2. Serve over a bed of rice. Drizzle with balsamic glaze before serving.

GRILLED SPAM CHEESE SANDWICH WITH BRIE AND PEACHES

INGREDIENTS:
- Eight pieces of sourdough bread.
- butter (four tablespoons, room temperature)
- 8 fluid ounces of Brie cheese, thinly sliced
- thinly sliced peaches (two huge ones)
- 4 tablespoons Dijon mustard (honey mustard)
- 1 can (12 ounces) of SPAM Less Sodium in a thinly sliced format

INSTRUCTIONS:
1. Preparing the grill for medium-high heat is essential.
2. Each side should be golden brown after approximately three minutes on the grill with the SPAM Less Sodium. Make a mental note to put it away.
3. Each piece of bread should be brushed with butter on one side. Assemble the sandwiches by starting with the bread butter side, adding the Brie, cooked SPAM Less Sodium, a smear of honey mustard, and finishing with the bread butter side again.
4. Place the sandwiches on a grill to cook. Toasted golden brown bread and melted cheese should take around three minutes to cook in the oven.

CRUNCHY NUGGETS MADE WITH SPAM

INGREDIENTS:
- 1 (12-ounce) can SPAM Classic (or similar)
- 6 cups of corn and oat cereal with added sugar
- 1 cup of all-purpose flour

- 4 eggs, lightly beaten
- a third cup of milk
- To use as a dipping sauce, maple syrup

INSTRUCTIONS:

1. Preheat the oven to 350 degrees Fahrenheit. Set aside the SPAM Classic, which has been cut into 16 equal-sized pieces.
2. Place cereal in a bowl and crush it until it resembles bread crumbs. In a second dish, whisk together the flour and salt. Mix the eggs and milk in a separate container until well combined and smooth.
3. Each SPAM piece should be dipped into the flour, then the egg/milk mixture. Repeat the process one more, and then liberally cover each with cereal. Place the baking sheet on top of it.
4. Baking for 20 minutes, or until golden and crisp, is recommended. Pieces should be turned approximately halfway through. Toss with maple syrup or your favorite dipping sauce before serving!

SPAM CLASSIC MAC & CHEESE IN A SINGLE SKILLET

INGREDIENTS:

- SPAM Classic (diced) from one 12-ounce can
- 4 cups whole milk (serves 2)
- 1.1/2 cups elbow macaroni that has not been cooked
- Two cups of mildly shredded cheese Cheddar cheese is a kind of cheese.
- 1/2 cup shredded part-skim mozzarella
- 2 ounces of cream cheese
- butter, divided into 4 tablespoons
- 1 teaspoon Dijon mustard

- a quarter teaspoon of cayenne pepper
- a pinch of ground nutmeg
- Panko bread crumbs
- 1 cup salt
- 1 teaspoon pepper
- if desired, 1 tablespoon of finely chopped parsley

INSTRUCTIONS:
1. Preheat the broiler to its highest setting.
2. Cook SPAM Classic for 2 to 3 minutes, or until lightly browned, in a large broiler-safe pan over medium-high heat until gently browned. Remove the skillet from the heat.
3. In the same skillet, cook the milk and macaroni over medium heat until the macaroni is hot. Bring the pot to a simmer. Prepare the macaroni for 5 to 6 minutes, constantly stirring to avoid sticking, or until it is soft and the sauce has thickened. Remove the pan from the heat. Combine the cheeses, 2 tablespoons butter, mustard, cayenne pepper, nutmeg, and salt in a large mixing bowl. Add in the browned SPAM Classic and mix well.
4. Melt the remaining 2 tablespoons of butter in a small microwave-safe bowl. Stir in the breadcrumbs until they are well coated. The mixture should be sprinkled on top of the macaroni and cheese.
5. Place the pan in the broiler for 3 to 5 minutes until the breadcrumbs are golden brown. Depending on your preference, garnish with parsley.

SPAM CLASSIC KIMBAP

INGREDIENTS:
- 3 cups sushi rice that has been cooked
- 8 sheets of nori seaweed

- 1 can (12 ounces) of SPAM Classic sliced into thin ribbons and sautéed
- 1 carrot, peeled and julienned
- slices of 1 cucumber cut into long strips, thinly sliced
- (2) 2 eggs, softly beaten, lightly fried, fried until crispy, and sliced into strips
- Baby spinach, sautéed and seasoned to taste 4 cups
- 8 slices of pickled radish (yellow)

INSTRUCTIONS:

1. One sheet of Nori should be placed in the work area. Moisten your hands and distribute the Rice evenly over the Nori, leaving a 1-inch strip of Nori exposed on one end.
2. SPAM is layered on top of everything else. Make a rollout of classic strips of beef and vegetables such as carrots, cucumber, egg strips, spinach, and pickled radish.
3. Using a tiny bit of water, moisten the end of the Nori to help it stick together.
4. Repeat the process with the remaining components.
5. Rolls should be cut into bite-sized pieces.

BUDAE JJIGAE ARMY STEW WITH SPAM

INGREDIENTS:

- 1 can (12 ounces) of SPAM Classic Pork and beans from a single 8-ounce can be sliced
- 7 ounces sliced Kielbasa (16-ounce) firm tofu, sliced
- 1 cup kimchi, diced
- 1/2 onion, cut
- 8 ounces mushrooms, sliced
- 1 package of firm tofu, sliced
- (4.2-ounce) package of Ramen noodle soup from Korea, with a flavor packet

- 2 tablespoons Korean chili flakes (Korean chili powder)
- 1/4 cup Korean chili paste
- 1 tablespoon minced garlic, if desired
- 2 tbsp soy sauce
- 12 tsp freshly ground black pepper
- 4 cups chicken broth
- 1 cup chopped green onions
- 4 cups chicken broth
- rice that has been cooked to a crisp

INSTRUCTIONS:

1. Cook the SPAM Classic slices in a large pan over medium-high heat for 3 to 5 minutes, or until they are browned.
2. Spread SPAM Classic slices on the bottom of a vast shallow pot or skillet. Add the pork and beans on top, followed by Kielbasa and tofu, along with onion and mushrooms. Place the ramen noodle on top of the sauce.
3. Combine the ramen spice package with the chili flakes, chili paste, garlic, soy sauce, and pepper in a small mixing dish.
4. Pour chicken stock over the spice combination in the saucepan and bring it to a boil.
5. Bring the saucepan to a boil over medium-high heat, then reduce the heat to low and simmer, constantly stirring, for 5 to 6 minutes, or until the noodles are soft and the stew is well heated. Garnish with green onions, if desired. Serve with a side of Rice.

MUSUBI WITH SPAM FOR BREAKFAST

INGREDIENTS:

- SPAM (four slices) Teriyaki
- HORMEL BLACK LABEL bacon, cut into 4 pieces
- 4 oz. shredded cheddar cheese
- Furikake

- 1 sheet nori seaweed
- 2 cups cooked Rice (uncooked)
- 3 quail eggs
- Mirin
- 1 teaspoon sugar
- 1 teaspoon salt
- the equivalent of two tablespoons of DASH

INSTRUCTIONS:

1. Cook the Rice and season it with mirin to your liking. Nori should be cut into four equal-sized strips.
2. Combine the following: eggs, sugar, 2 tablespoons of mirin, a bit of salt, and dashi (not required). Using a vigorous whisk, combine the ingredients. A pan (ideally one with a heavy bottom, one made of cast iron, or a rectangular Tamago pan) should be heated to medium heat with evenly distributed oil. Pour one-third of the egg mixture into the pan and cook until set. Once the egg begins to set, fold it over upon itself like an omelet and turn it over. Simple egg pancakes may be made using the same egg mixture and only need to be flipped once. Repeat the process with the remaining egg.
3. Using a sharp knife, cut the tomato into four equal pieces. Form the sushi rice into four rectangular blocks using a musubi mold or a baking sheet to prevent it from sticking together (pushing the Rice into a corner of the baking sheet with a rice paddle). Furikake should be poured onto a plate and used to cover the whole surface of each block of Rice with furikake.
4. Place the block of Rice (which has now been coated with furikake) on the ground. Place a piece of cheddar cheese on top of the Rice, followed by bacon, Tamago (egg combination), and sautéed SPAM teriyaki (SPAM in a sauce). Wrap the two ends below the block of Rice with a strip of Nori and fasten with a knot in the middle.

BAKED FRENCH TOAST WITH SPAM

INGREDIENTS:

- 1 (12-ounce) can SPAM with Real Hormel Bacon, cubed
- 1 (16-ounce) loaf of Hawaiian sliced bread, diced into 1-inch pieces
- 1 (12-ounce) can SPAM with Real Hormel Bacon, cubed
- 8 quail eggs
- 1 cup half-and-half (or cream)
- 1 cup coconut milk
- 1 cup pineapple chunks, drained and crushed
- 1/2 cup toasted sweetened flaked coconut, cut into pieces

INSTRUCTIONS:

1. Preheat the oven to 350 degrees Fahrenheit. Prepare a 9-by-13-inch baking dish by lightly greasing it.
2. Cook SPAM with Bacon in a big pan over medium heat for 2 to 3 minutes, or until gently browned, then remove from heat and put aside to cool.
3. To assemble, spread the bread cubes in the prepared pan and top with SPAM and bacon.
4. Whisk the eggs, half-and-half, and coconut milk in a large mixing bowl. Combine the crushed pineapple and half of the sweetened flaked coconut in a large mixing bowl. Pour over the SPAM with Bacon in an equal layer. To help the bread absorb the egg mixture, press it down gently.
5. Bake for 30 minutes with the oven door ajar. Sprinkle with the remaining coconut flakes for fifteen minutes or until the coconut is toasted.

SANDWICH WITH SPAM ON A BAGEL

INGREDIENTS:

- Two slices of SPAM with Real Hormel Bacon.
- 2 tablespoons melted butter, slightly softened
- 1. Everything bagel, cut in half
- 1 piece of smoked American cheese
- 1 fried egg, over easy, cooked in a skillet
- Arugula leaves, tomato slices, and red onion are used as toppings.

INSTRUCTIONS:
1. Preheat the oven to 350°F and cook the SPAM with Bacon according to package Instructions until browned.
2. Baste the sliced sides of the bagel with melted butter. Toast until the bread is golden brown.
3. Top the bottom half of the bagel with SPAM, bacon pieces, cheese, and an egg. Add chosen toppings and the other half of the bagel on top.

FRIED SPAMBALL SERVED WITH SPICY RANCH DRESSING

INGREDIENTS:
- 2 cups chopped SPAM Classic, diced
- 2 cups sushi quality rice that has been cooked
- 1 cup shredded mozzarella cheese, preferably fresh
- 1/2 cup parsley, finely chopped
- a half-cup of Nori shredded
- a half-cup of nori powder
- 1 tablespoon gochujang (Chinese chili paste) (Korean pepper paste)
- Cayenne pepper
- 1 teaspoon garlic powder
- 1 teaspoon onion powder

- 1 tablespoon sesame seeds
- Sesame oil (around a tablespoon)
- 1 quail (egg)
- season with salt and pepper to taste
- 2 cups panko breadcrumbs

INSTRUCTIONS:
1. Heat the frying oil to 360 degrees Fahrenheit.
2. In a large mixing bowl, combine all ingredients except the breadcrumbs and thoroughly mix them.
3. Roll the mixture into 1.1/2-inch rice balls with your hands.
4. Spread the panko crumbs and 2 tablespoons of minced parsley on a big dish and mix well.
5. Roll the rice balls in panko crumbs to coat them.
6. Using a deep-fryer, cook the rice balls till golden brown.
7. Place on a platter lined with paper towels to cool.
8. Prepare a serving dish by placing the cooled rice ball on it and garnishing it with spicy ranch and nori powder.

SPAM SLIDER WITH A BLOODY MARY FLAVOUR

INGREDIENTS:
- 1-(12-ounce) can of SPAM Classic.
- 1 cup ketchup
- 2 tablespoons horseradish, drained and minced
- one-and-a-half tablespoons Worcestershire sauce
- a half teaspoon of spicy sauce
- Celery is a vegetable that grows in a bunch of different ways (finely diced)
- Pickles are a kind of cucumber (sliced)

INSTRUCTIONS:

1. Ketchup, horseradish, Worcestershire sauce, and spicy sauce should all be mixed. Refrigerate for at least 1 hour before serving.
2. Cut the SPAM Classic into pieces that will fit on the slider buns and fry on the griddle until golden brown, about 2 minutes on each side.
3. Bloody Mary Ketchup should be spread on the slider buns.
4. Buns should be stuffed with SPAM Classic, then topped with celery and pickles.

EGGS WITH SPAM CHEESY TOAST

INGREDIENTS:
- 6 corn tortillas, every 6 inches in diameter
- 2 teaspoons of melted butter
- 1 (12-ounce) can SPAM Classic (cut into 24 pieces), drained
- 6 giant eggs (about)
- 2 cups queso fresco cheese in powder form
- 2 tbsp. vegetable oil
- Salsa of your choice to serve as a topping

INSTRUCTIONS:
1. Heat the oil in a frying pan. Fry the tortillas in hot oil as quickly as possible. Using paper towels, dry thoroughly.
2. In the same frying pan, cook the eggs in the butter over medium heat until done. Take the eggs out of the pan. Fry till golden brown on both sides after adding the SPAM.
3. Place 4 slices of fried SPAM on each tortilla, then top with a fried egg to complete the dish. Sprinkle with a third of a cup of cheese. Spread the salsa of your choice on top of the word.

CORNDOG WITH LONO SPAM

INGREDIENTS:

- 2-pack (12-ounce) SPAM Classic, peeled and deveined
- 12 ounces rock shrimp, peeled and deveined
- 1/2 cup finely sliced green onion
- 2 teaspoons minced ginger
- 1/2 cup finely chopped garlic
- 4 garlic cloves, peeled and minced
- 1 tablespoon Japanese 7-Spice (Shichimi) spice (around 1 tablespoon total)
- 1 tablespoon soy sauce
- 1.1/2 tablespoons freshly ground white pepper
- Plastic food wrap is 12 × 12 inches (eight sheets).
- a total of eight skewers
- 6 quarts of vegetable oil for deep-frying
- 1 cup of all-purpose flour
- 1 cup ground cornmeal
- Baking powder (about 2 teaspoons)
- 1 teaspoon of table salt
- 1 tbsp. table sugar
- 2 tablespoons shortening (vegetable oil)
- 1 gallon of milk
- 1 quail (egg)
- the equivalent of 2 tablespoons of Furikake spice
- Ketchup made from bananas, to be used for serving

INSTRUCTIONS:

1. Place SPAM Classic and shrimp in a food processor bowl and pulse until smooth. Pulse a few times to chop the ingredients finely. Into a large mixing basin, add the remaining ingredients. Mix in the green onion, ginger, garlic, 7-spice, soy sauce, and white pepper until everything is evenly distributed.

2. One sheet of food wrap should be placed in the work area—place 1/2 cup of the SPAM mixture on top of that. Carefully roll the plastic wrap into a sausage form, twisting the ends together to seal it. Make a total of 12 sausages by repeating the process.
3. Two cups of water should be brought to a boil in a big pan over high heat. Cover the sausages in a bamboo steamer in the pan with a lid—steam for 10 minutes with the lid on. Remove from heat and chill for 30 minutes or until cool, wrapped in plastic wrap. Remove the plastic wrap from the food. Each sausage should have a skewer inserted into one end.
4. Heat the oil in a big saucepan over medium-high heat until it reaches 375°F.
5. Combine the flour, cornmeal, baking powder, salt, and sugar in a large mixing basin. I used a fork and cut in the shortening. Stir in the milk and egg until everything is well-combined. Add in the Furikake and mix well. Fill a tall container halfway with the batter.
6. Dip the SPAM skewers into the batter, allowing excess to drop down the sides.
7. Working in batches, carefully put the battered SPAM skewers into the heated oil and fry for 3 to 4 minutes, until golden brown and crispy. Using paper towels, soak up the excess liquid.
8. Serve with banana ketchup on the side.

SPAM CLASSIC AND BEEF RAMEN

INGREDIENTS:
- a box of Ramen noodle soup with beef taste (three three-ounce containers)
- 6 fried eggs 1 (12-ounce) can SPAM Classic, sliced
- 1 baked potato
- 1/2 cup chopped green onions

INSTRUCTIONS:

1. Cook the noodles according to the package instructions, including the spice packet.
2. Individual serving bowls of ramen should be divided among six people.
3. Cook SPAM Classic in a big pan over medium-high heat for 2 to 3 minutes, or until it begins to brown.
4. Add sliced SPAM Classic, a fried egg, and green onions to the ramen and broth to finish it off.

SANDWICHES WITH SPAM AND CHEESE

INGREDIENTS:
- 1 (12-ounce) can SPAM Classic, split into 8 equal portions
- 8 pieces of swiss cheese
- 8 slices of bread, lightly toasted

INSTRUCTIONS:
1. Cook the SPAM Classic in a large pan over medium-high heat for 3 to 5 minutes, or until it is browned.
2. Cook for 1 to 2 minutes, or until the cheese is melted, on top of the pieces of bread.
3. Serve on a slice of toasted bread.

TACOS WITH SPAM

INGREDIENTS:
- SPAM Classic, split into strips from 1 (12-ounce) can
- 1 small onion, diced

- 1/2 cup cilantro, finely chopped
- salsa for serving 1 (10-count) box of taco-size corn tortillas that have been warmed

INSTRUCTIONS:

1. Cook the SPAM Classic in a large pan over medium-high heat for 3 to 5 minutes, or until it is lightly browned.
2. Fill tortillas with SPAM Classic and top with onion and cilantro. Serve with a side of salsa.

SUMMER ROLLS WITH SPAM

INGREDIENTS:

- 1 can (12 ounces) of SPAM Cut into tiny strips; this is a classic.
- 2 tbsp soy sauce
- 1 cup sugar (or 2 teaspoons)
- 3-ounce bag of steamed main rice stick noodles (angel hair-style)
- 8 (8-inch) round spring roll spring rolls wrappers made of rice paper
- 1/2 cucumber, thinly sliced
- 1 carrot, peeled and julienned
- There are four leaves. The spines were removed from bibb lettuce to create eight half leaves.
- peanuts that have been chopped
- slices of lime
- Sauce for peanuts made using SKIPPY Creamy Peanut Butter and rice vinegar (3/4 cup total)
- 1/3 cup soy sauce
- three teaspoons of honey
- 1 and a half tablespoons of freshly grated ginger
- 1 garlic clove, peeled and minced
- 1/4 teaspoon red pepper flakes

- *2 teaspoons of distilled water*

INSTRUCTIONS:

1. Two tablespoons of soy sauce and 2 teaspoons of sugar are combined in a small mixing basin.
2. Cook the SPAM Classic strips for 3 to 5 minutes, or until they are browned, in a large pan over medium-high heat. Immediately add the soy sauce and sugar mixture and simmer for 1 to 2 minutes, or until slices are glazed, before removing from the heat.
3. Cook the rice stick noodles for 2 to 3 minutes, or until they are soft yet firm, in a kettle of boiling water. Drain well after rinsing under cold running water.
4. To construct the rolls, fill a 10-inch glass pie dish halfway with boiling water and set it aside. Place 1 rice wrapper in the water and let it sit for 2 to 3 seconds, or just long enough to become malleable, before removing it from the water. Place the rice wrapper on a level surface so it can be easily folded. Fill the bottom third of the wrapper with SPAM Classic, rice noodles, cucumber, and carrot, then fold the wrapper over.
5. One piece of lettuce should be folded in half and placed on top. Fold the bottom of the wrapper up over the Ingredients, then fold in the sides, and then continue rolling up the wrapper as before. Spread a moist paper towel on a plate and place the roll seam-side down to prevent it from drying.
6. Continue with the remaining rice wrappers and filling Ingredients until all are used.
7. The SKIPPY Creamy Peanut Butter, the rice vinegar, the 1/3 cup soy sauce, the honey, the ginger, the garlic, the red pepper flakes, and the water are combined to form the dipping sauce, which may be served with the chicken or with the vegetables.
8. Cut the spring rolls in half and serve them with the dipping sauce as a first dish.

CLASSIC BIBIMBAP BOWL WITH SPAM

INGREDIENTS:

- chopped from 1 (12-ounce) can of SPAM Classic
- 2 garlic cloves, peeled and minced
- 2 tablespoons sesame oil
- 1 tablespoon soy sauce
- Divide 2 tablespoons of vegetable oil in half.
- Bean sprouts (1.1/2 cups)
- roughly cut 4 cups of young baby spinach leaves
- 4 cups of hot-cooked Rice
- 1 carrot, julienned
- 1 carrot, grated
- 1 cup kimchi (Korean pickled vegetables)
- 4 eggs, fried to a crisp
- 4 tablespoons gochujang (distributed evenly)
- Toasted sesame seeds

INSTRUCTIONS:

1. Combine the garlic, sesame oil, and soy sauce in a small mixing bowl.
2. Heat 2 teaspoons vegetable oil in a large pan over medium-high heat until shimmering.
3. Pour in the bean sprouts and a third of the garlic mixture and stir-fry for 1 to 2 minutes, or until the nodes are crisp-tender. Remove the pan from the heat.
4. Heat 2 tablespoons of additional vegetable oil in the same pan over medium-high heat until shimmering.
5. In the same skillet, add spinach and another third of the garlic mixture; stir-fry for 1 to 2 minutes, or until spinach has wilted. Remove the pan from the heat.
6. Heat the remaining oil in the same skillet over medium-high heat until shimmering. Stir in the carrots and the remaining garlic mixture for 1 to 2 minutes, or until the carrots are crisp-tender. Remove the pan from the heat.

7. Cook the SPAM Classic for 2 to 3 minutes, or until it is browned and crisp, in the same pan over medium-high heat. Remove the pan from the heat.
8. To assemble the dish, divide the cooked Rice into four words. Bean sprouts, spinach, carrots, SPAM Classic, kimchi, egg, gochujang, and sesame seeds are sprinkled on each bowl.

GYROS WITH SPAM

INGREDIENTS:
- 1 (12-ounce) can of SPAM (per person) Classic, but thinly sliced
- 1 (12-ounce) can think of SPAM (per person) Oven Roasted turkey breast, thinly sliced
- 2 cups plain Greek yogurt (not flavored)
- Peel and seed 1 cucumber, then shred it finely.
- 2 teaspoons freshly squeezed lemon juice
- 1 teaspoon garlic powder
- 1/2 teaspoon dill weed (dry, ground)
- one-and-a-half teaspoons of salt
- peppercorns (1/4 teaspoon)
- 8 pita bread rounds.
- Toppings such as shredded lettuce, sliced tomato, chopped red onion, diced cucumbers, and feta cheese are recommended.

INSTRUCTIONS:
1. Cook the SPAM Classic and SPAM Oven Roasted Turkey in batches in a large pan over medium-high heat for 2 to 3 minutes for each set, or until gently browned and crisped, about 2 to 3 minutes total. After that, lay it away.
2. Combine the yogurt, cucumber, lemon juice, garlic powder, salt, and pepper in a medium-sized mixing bowl until well blended.

3. Place the SPAM Classic and the SPAM Oven Roasted Turkey on the pita rounds and serve immediately. Serve with a dollop of the yogurt mixture. To finish, add the indicated toppings.

KABOBS MADE WITH SPAM TERIYAKI, PINEAPPLE, AND RED PEPPERS

INGREDIENTS:
- 1 can of SPAM (12 ounces) Cubed Teriyaki marinated with soy sauce
- 1 red bell pepper, peeled and cut into 3/4-inch chunks
- 1 red onion, peeled and sliced into wedges 3/4 inch thick
- 2 cups pineapple chunks (fresh or frozen)
- a third of a cup of teriyaki sauce

INSTRUCTIONS:
1. Preheat the grill to a medium setting.
2. Alternately thread the SPAM Teriyaki, bell pepper, onion, and pineapple onto 8 to 12 skewers, leaving space between each.
3. Grill the skewers, turning them periodically and coating them with teriyaki sauce, for 8 minutes, or until the kabobs are hot and the grill markings are thick and noticeable.

TACOS WITH SPAM A LA BARBACOA CON JALAPENOS Y SALSA DE PINEAPPLE

INGREDIENTS:
- 1 can (12 ounces) of SPAM a jalapeno pepper, chopped

- 1/2 cup pineapple, cut into cubes (you may use a can if fresh is not available)
- 1/4 cup finely diced onions
- 10 corn tortillas that have been heated
- 1 sprig of cilantro leaves (fresh)
- 1 jalapeno, peeled and diced
- 1 lime
- 1 avocado
- 1 cup cotija cheese
- 1/2 cup guacamole
- a half-cup of sour cream
- a third cup of barbecue sauce
- Adding hot sauce to taste is optional.

INSTRUCTIONS:

1. Pineapple Salsa may be made by combining the pineapple, cilantro, onion, Jalapeno, and half of the lime juice in a small mixing dish and mixing well. Season with salt and pepper to taste, and then put the pan aside.
2. Another small bowl should be used for this and mashed with a fork before adding the sour cream and the juice of one remaining half lime. Adjust seasonings with salt and pepper to taste and leave away.
3. Sauté the SPAM Jalapeno in a large pan until it is lightly browned. Stir in the barbecue sauce for 2 minutes, then remove from heat and set aside.
4. Preparing the tortilla: Heat it according to the package guidelines, then spoon in the avocado crema and SPAM Jalapeo combination.
5. If desired, tacos may be topped with Pineapple Salsa, cheese, and fresh cilantro. If desired, top with spicy sauce before serving.

SPAM SLAW WITH NOODLES IN AN ASIAN STYLE

INGREDIENTS:
- 1 can (12 ounces) of SPAM Sodium-reduced, diced
- 1 box ramen noodles (about 3 ounces), cooked and cooled (discard the seasoning packet or use to season soup)
- chopped coleslaw mix (one 12-ounce package)
- 1 (8-ounce) container of frozen edamame-shelled soybeans (edamame is a soybean).
- 1/2 cup slivered almonds
- 5 tablespoons green onions, finely sliced
- Asian Honey is a kind of honey from Asia. Vinaigrette:
- SKIPPY Creamy Peanut Butter (about a third cup)
- a third of a cup of honey
- rice vinegar (about a third of a cup)
- 2 tablespoons soy sauce
- Sesame oil (around a tablespoon)
- to taste, 1 tablespoon water, 1 teaspoon salt, 1 teaspoon pepper

INSTRUCTIONS:
1. Set aside in a large mixing bowl once you have combined all the ingredients for the Asian Honey Vinaigrette dressing.
2. Cook SPAM Less Sodium in a big pan until crisp and gently browned, about 5 minutes. Remove from frying and put aside.
3. Cook the ramen noodles according to the package instructions; drain and put aside.
4. In a large mixing bowl, add the SPAM Less Sodium, the noodles, the coleslaw, the edamame, the almonds, the green onions, and the green onions. Stir in the dressing until everything is well-combined.
5. Refrigerate for a few hours or overnight until ready to serve.

MUSUBI WITH TERIYAKI AND TAKUAN SPAM

INGREDIENTS:

- 12-ounce can SPAM Teriyaki, cut into 8 slices by cutting it lengthwise.
- ounces of white steamed Rice that has been prepared ahead of time
- cut in half 4 sheets of Japanese Nori (seaweed)
- 1-ounce extra-virgin olive oil
- 1 tbsp. freshly squeezed ginger root juice
- 4 tbsp. Yamasa soy sauce
- 1/4 cup water
- 2 tablespoons of cane sugar (brown)
- half an ounce of green onion whites, peeled and split in half, lengthwise
- Takuan (pickled daikon) that has been pre-purchased

INSTRUCTIONS:

1. The SPAM Teriyaki should be cooked until it has a good sear on both sides before being removed from the pan and placed on one side.
2. In the same pan, combine the soy sauce, water, ginger juice, sugar, and green onion, and bring to a simmer over medium heat.
3. Then, return the SPAM Teriyaki to the pan and allow it to simmer in the sauce for 3-4 minutes.
4. Remove the SPAM Teriyaki from the pan and lay it over the Rice before wrapping it with Nori.
5. Add the Takuan that has been chopped (or pickled daikon)—warm the dish before serving.

POKE BOWL WITH SPAM

INGREDIENTS:
- 1 can (12 ounces) of SPAM diced teriyaki sauce
- 1 cup sushi rice
- 1 cup edamame beans, shelled
- 2 medium avocados, diced
- 1/2 cup shredded carrots
- 1/4 cup pickled ginger
- 4 finely sliced green onions
- 2 teaspoons rice vinegar.
- 1 tablespoon freshly squeezed lime juice
- 1 tablespoon light soy sauce
- Sesame oil (around a tablespoon)
- To finish, add a sprinkle of black sesame seeds.

INSTRUCTIONS:
1. Cook the Rice according to the instructions on the box.
2. Distribute the Rice into four serving dishes in a uniform layer.
3. Cook the SPAM Teriyaki according to the package instructions until it is browned on the outside.
4. Distribute the SPAM Teriyaki among the rice bowls in a uniform layer.
5. Add the edamame, avocado, shredded carrots, pickled ginger, and green onions.
6. In a small mixing bowl, whisk together the rice vinegar, lime juice, soy sauce, and sesame oil until well combined and smooth.
7. Drizzle the dressing over the rice bowls and garnish with sesame seeds if used.

CUBAN SPAMWICH, FRESHLY PRESSED IN A HOT PRESS

INGREDIENTS:

- Three ounces SPAM Classic, thinly cut using a meat slicer.
- 1 soft French roll (6 inches in diameter)
- 2 tablespoons of unsalted butter, melted and softened
- thinly slice the lengthwise length of 2 ounces of kosher dill pickle
- Swiss cheese, finely sliced (about 2 ounces)
- 2 tablespoons hot prepared mustard

INSTRUCTIONS:

1. Preheat a flattop grill or panini press to 375°F, or medium-high, depending on your preference.
2. To make the SPAM Classic sandwich, cut the roll in half and spread 1 ounce of cheese on the bottom half. Next, stack the thinly sliced SPAM Classic on top, folding it as you go down the bread.
3. Pickle slices and the remaining 1 ounce of cheese should be placed on top of the SPAM Classic.
4. Spread the mustard on the roll, then lay the roll on top of the sandwich and close the sandwich.
5. Brush the remaining butter on both sides of the bread and lay it on the grill for 2 minutes to toast it up. Firmly push down on the sandwich as it is being grilled.
6. After the first side has gone golden brown and crispy, flip the sandwich over and cook for another 2 to 3 minutes, pushing down on it the whole time.

BAKED HASHBROWNS WITH SPAM

INGREDIENTS:

- 12-ounce can SPAM Classic (cut into cubes), drained and rinsed

- *1/2 cup melted butter or margarine*
- *1 (10.75-ounce) can of cream chicken soup*
- *1/2 cup finely chopped onion*
- *1/2 cup finely chopped garlic*
- *2 cups drained and crumbled potato chips*
- *One can of green chiles (about 2 ounces) drained and chopped.*
- *1 frozen hashbrown potato packet (32 ounces) that has been partially thawed*
- *garlic powder (half a teaspoon)*
- *a half-gallon of milk*
- *1 teaspoon freshly ground pepper*
- *1 teaspoon of table salt*
- *Two cups of shredded beef Cheddar cheese is a kind of cheese.*
- *1.1/2 cups sour cream*

INSTRUCTIONS:

1. Preheat the oven to 350 degrees Fahrenheit.
2. In a large mixing basin, add the potatoes, the butter, the salt, the pepper, and the garlic powder; thoroughly incorporate.
3. A big mixing dish should combine the cheese, SPAM Classic (or other flavorings), soup (or other Ingredients), sour cream, milk, onion, and chilies. Add to the potato mixture and combine well. Pour the mixture into a 2-quart baking dish. Crush the chips and sprinkle on top.
4. Bake for 45 to 60 minutes, or until the dish is well heated.

SPAM WITH SCALLOPED POTATOES

INGREDIENTS:

- *SPAM Classic, thinly sliced from a 12-ounce can*
- *all-purpose flour (three tablespoons)*
- *3 tablespoons of butter or other fatty substance*

- *breadcrumbs (1/2 cup) that have been crisped in butter*
- *potatoes, cooked and sliced (four huge potatoes)*
- *2 quarts of milk*
- *1 tablespoon finely minced fresh parsley*
- *pepper, according to personal preference*
- *season with salt to taste*
- *1 small onion, peeled and chopped*

INSTRUCTIONS:

1. Preheat the oven to 375 degrees Fahrenheit.
2. Melt the butter in a skillet over medium heat, then whisk in the flour, salt, and pepper.
3. Cook for 3 to 4 minutes on low heat, stirring regularly until the sauce has thickened.
4. Combine the onion, parsley, and milk in a large mixing bowl.
5. Cook, constantly stirring, until the sauce has thickened somewhat.
6. Create layers of potato and SPAM Classic in a casserole by layering them alternately.
7. Pour the white sauce over the top and sprinkle with breadcrumbs to finish it off.
8. Preheat the oven to 300°F and bake for 30 minutes.

BENEDICT, THE SPAM BENEDICT

INGREDIENTS:

- *1 (12-ounce) can SPAM Classic (or similar)*
- *1 cup melted butter*
- *4 egg yolks*
- *4 English muffins that have been divided and lightly toasted*
- *a half cup of fresh spinach*
- *8 big quail eggs*
- *3.1/2 teaspoons freshly squeezed lemon juice*

- Tomatoes cut into 8 pieces
- 1 tablespoon of distilled water
- 1 teaspoon white vinegar

INSTRUCTIONS:
1. The Hollandaise sauce is made by partially filling a double boiler with water, ensuring the water does not touch the top of the broiler pan.
2. Bring the water to a gentle boil.
3. In the top of a double-boiler, whisk together the egg yolks, lemon juice, and 1 tablespoon of water until well combined and smooth.
4. Whisk continually as you add the butter to the egg yolk mixture, about 1 or 2 tablespoons at a time. If the sauce gets too thick, add 1 to 2 tablespoons of hot water until it thins out. Whisk until all of the butter has been integrated.
5. Remove the pan from the heat and cover it with aluminum foil.
6. To poach the eggs, fill a big saucepan halfway with water and bring it to a boil.
7. Add vinegar once the water has been brought to a moderate simmer.
8. To cook the eggs, carefully break them into the boiling water and cook for 2 1/2 to 3 minutes, or until the whites are set, but the yolks are still soft in the middle. Remove the eggs using a slotted spoon and place them on a heated dish.
9. Meanwhile, cut the SPAM Classic into four slices that are 1/4 inch thick.
10. Heat SPAM Classic in a medium pan over medium-high heat until it is gently crisped, about 3 minutes.
11. Cut-side-up English muffins should be placed on serving platters.
12. Top with spinach, SPAM Classic, tomato, and a poached egg, dividing them equally. Hollandaise sauce should be drizzled on top. If desired, garnish with chopped chives. Serve as soon as possible.

PIZZA ROLLS WITH SPAM

INGREDIENTS:
- 1 (12-ounce) can SPAM Classic (or similar)
- garlic powder (half a teaspoon)
- grated Parmesan cheese (about 2 tablespoons)
- One teaspoon of dry Italian seasoning.
- 1/4 cup extra-virgin olive oil (plus more for brushing dough)
- 1 (11-ounce) can of pizza crust from the refrigerator (thin style)
- 1 (8-ounce) box of shredded mozzarella cheese (finely shredded)
- To use as a dipping sauce for pizza

INSTRUCTIONS:
1. Preheat the oven to 400 degrees Fahrenheit.
2. Add olive oil to a small bowl and stir in the garlic powder, Parmesan cheese, Italian seasoning, and pepper. Make a mental note to put it away.
3. Prepare a rimmed baking sheet by lining it with aluminum foil and gently spraying it with cooking spray.
4. Remove the pizza dough from the container and place it on a piece of aluminum foil.
5. Cut the dough into three long strips using a tiny knife and set aside.
6. Lightly brush the tops of the strips with olive oil to seal the moisture.
7. To prepare the SPAM Classic, cut it into quarter-inch slices and then in half lengthwise.
8. Place the SPAM slices in two rows along the length of each dough strip, one row on each side of the dough strip.
9. Each dough strip should have a third of the cheese sprinkled on top.
10. Take each dough strip and roll it together until it forms a long log, starting at the long end. Continue moving until the seam is at the bottom.
11. Lightly brush the logs with olive oil to prevent them from drying out.
12. Bake for 12 minutes or until the top is lightly golden.

13. Remove the pan from the oven and coat the tops with garlic.
14. Return the pan to the oven for another 5 to 8 minutes, or until the top is lightly browned.
15. Allow for a 10-minute cooling period.
16. Using a cutting board, transfer the pizza rolls and cut them into 1.1/2-inch pieces. Serve immediately with a side of pizza sauce for dipping if desired.

SPAM CANTONESE SWEET AND SOUR

INGREDIENTS:
- 12-ounce can of SPAM Classic (cut into 1/2-inch pieces), drained, and set aside.
- 1 (8-ounce) can of bamboo shoots that have been exhausted.
- 1 carrot, finely cut across the grain diagonally
- 1 garlic clove, peeled and minced
- 1 tablespoon cornstarch
- 1 cucumber, peeled and sliced into 1/2-inch cubes
- 1 bunch of green onions, thinly chopped into quarter-inch pieces
- 1 teaspoon freshly grated ginger
- ketchup (three tablespoons)
- 1 teaspoon soy sauce
- 3 teaspoons of table sugar
- 2 tbsp. vegetable oil
- 3 tablespoons white wine vinegar
- a third cup of water

INSTRUCTIONS:
1. Heat the oil in a wok or big pan over medium heat until shimmering.
2. Cook for 4 to 5 minutes, occasionally stirring, until the carrots and onions are crisp-tender, and until the garlic is fragrant.

3. Cook for 5 to 6 minutes, or until the sauce has thickened, after adding the following 7 Ingredients to the skillet.
4. Combine SPAM Classic, bamboo shoots, and cucumber in a large mixing bowl.
5. Cook until the food is well warm. Serve over a bed of heated Rice.

ICE CREAM WITH MAPLE AND BROWN SUGAR SPAM.

INGREDIENTS:
- Spam with real HORMEL Bacon in a 12-ounce can
- a half cup of pure maple syrup
- a half cup of brown sugar
- 1 teaspoon pure vanilla extract
- 2 quarts of thick cream
- 2 quarts of milk
- 3/4 cup granulated sugar
- 2 teaspoons bourbon vanilla bean extract
- a pinch of salt

INSTRUCTIONS:
1. Slice the SPAM and Real HORMEL Bacon into 1/4-inch cubes before assembling the dish.
2. Brown sugar, maple syrup, and vanilla extract should be combined in a big pan.
3. Cook over medium heat until the sauce bubbles; lower heat to low and continue to stir until the sauce has been reduced by approximately one-third. Allow for cooling of the SPAM mixture.
4. Whisk together the cream, milk, bourbon, vanilla, and salt in a large mixing basin. Stir in the sugar until it is completely dissolved.
5. Placing the mixture in an ice cream freezer and freezing it according to the manufacturer's recommendations is

recommended. Pour the mixture into a storage container as soon as it has frozen but is still soft.
6. Freeze the ice cream for approximately an hour, then fold in the SPAM mixture, mixing it into the ice cream until it is completely incorporated. PLEASE DO NOT OVERMIX!
7. Place the container in the freezer to harden. This recipe serves 8.

CASSEROLE DE PIZZA CON SPAM

INGREDIENTS:
- Cut two (12-ounce) cans of SPAM oven-roasted turkey into 1/2-inch pieces and set them.
- 1 can (about 10.75 ounces) Soup with cheddar cheese
- 6-cups defrosted and thawed frozen shredded hashbrown potatoes
- 1 large egg that has been gently beaten
- (1/4-pound) canned mushroom stems and pieces, drained
- 1 onion, chopped
- 1/4 teaspoon freshly ground pepper
- 14-16-ounce jar pizza sauce (about)
- a half teaspoon of salt
- Four cups shredded pizza cheese mix.
- 1 tablespoon of extra-virgin olive oil

INSTRUCTIONS:
1. Preheat the oven to 400 degrees Fahrenheit.
2. Prepare a 15x10x1-inch baking pan with cooking spray.
3. In a medium-sized mixing basin, add the potatoes, soup, egg, salt, and pepper; thoroughly blend.
4. Pour the mixture onto the baking pan and spread it out evenly.
5. Baking time is 20 to 22 minutes, or until the top is gently browned.

6. Meanwhile, heat the oil in a large pan over medium heat until shimmering.
7. Combine the SPAM Oven Roasted Turkey, onion, and mushrooms in a large mixing bowl.
8. Cook for 5 to 8 minutes, or until the bottom of the pan is gently browned.
9. Add in the pizza sauce and mix well.
10. Two cups of cheese should be sprinkled over the heated potato crust.
11. To finish, sprinkle the SPAM mixture and the remaining 2 cups of cheese.
12. Bake for 5 to 7 minutes until the cheese is melted and the crust is golden brown.
13. Cut the pizza into squares using a pizza cutter.

EGG ROLLS WITH SPAM-YUM FILLING

INGREDIENTS:
- 1 can (12 ounces) of SPAM With Real HORMEL Bacon, which has been coarsely diced
- Half a cup habanero pepper jelly (or other favorite hot jellies), halved 1 cup vegetable oil, split 4 teaspoons soy sauce (or other favorite sweet and sour sauce), divided 6 tablespoons sugar, divided 4 cups shredded coleslaw, combine
- 12 egg roll wrappers
- 1/4 cup pureed pineapple (fresh or canned)

INSTRUCTIONS:
1. Preparation: Heat a nonstick pan over medium heat and cook the SPAM With Real HORMEL Bacon for 2 minutes, or until the SPAM is slightly crisped.

2. Stir in 1/4 cup of the pepper jelly until everything is well-combined, then put the mixture aside.
3. In a second nonstick pan, heat a tablespoon of oil with 2 teaspoons of soy sauce, 2 tablespoons of sweet and sour, 4 tablespoons of sugar, and the coleslaw mix until the soy sauce is hot and the sugar is dissolved.
4. Cook for approximately 1 minute over medium-high heat, or until the cabbage is slightly softened; remove from heat and put aside.
5. Place the egg roll wrappers on a platter and set them aside. Two tablespoons of the SPAM combination and 2 tablespoons of the coleslaw mixture should be placed in the middle of the plate.
6. Using a little water around the tip, seal the edges of the wrapper after folding and rolling it up.
7. Continue with the remaining egg roll wrappers and fill until all ingredients are used.
8. Heat the remaining vegetable oil in a deep fryer or a large deep pan over medium-high heat until it reaches 350° to 375°F.
9. Deep-fry egg rolls on both sides until golden brown, then take them from the oil and lay them on a cooling rack or paper towels to drain.
10. Blend the pineapple puree with the remaining soy sauce, sugar, and habanero jelly in a blender until the liquid has the consistency of a dipping sauce and is smooth. This recipe serves 12.

MEATBALLS WITH SPAM FROM THE FAR EAST AS AN APPETIZER

INGREDIENTS:
- 1 (12-ounce) can SPAM Classic (or similar)
- 1/4 cup + 1/3 cup finely chopped green onions, equal portions
- Bean sprouts, cut, and well-drained, 1/2 cup

- *a third cup of dried breadcrumbs*
- *1/4 cup finely chopped green bell pepper*
- *1/2 teaspoon freshly grated ginger, split*
- *1/2 cup tomato juice*

INSTRUCTIONS:
1. Preheat the oven to 425 degrees Fahrenheit.
2. Process the SPAM Classic in a food processor until it is finely diced or ground by hand in a mixing basin.
3. Stir well in the SPAM Classic, breadcrumbs, bean sprouts, 1/4 cup onions, 1/4 teaspoon ginger, and black pepper in a large mixing bowl until everything is well-combined.
4. Form the mixture into 24 meatballs, using about 1 tablespoon of the Ingredients for each meatball.
5. Bake for 15 minutes at 350°F on a wire rack in a shallow baking pan, then let cool to room temperature before serving.
6. To prepare the sauce, place the tomato juice, bell pepper, remaining 1/3 cup onions, and 1/4 teaspoon ginger in a small saucepan and heat over medium heat until warm.
7. Bring the water to a boil, then reduce the heat to a simmer for 5 minutes.
8. Cocktail picks are used to spear the meatballs. Prepare a warm sauce for dipping and serve with the dish.

VEGGIE SKEWERS WITH SPAM

INGREDIENTS:
- *1 (12-ounce) can SPAM Jalapeno, cut into pieces 1 cup shredded cheese*
- *2 teaspoons of melted butter*
- *2 teaspoons finely chopped fresh cilantro*
- *One red bell pepper, peeled and chopped into 3/4-inch chunks.*

- 1 red onion, peeled and cut into 3/4-inch-thick wedges
- 1 zucchini, peeled and cut into 3/4-inch chunks

INSTRUCTIONS:
1. Preheat the grill to a medium setting.
2. Using 8 to 12 skewers, alternately thread the SPAM Jalapeno, bell pepper, zucchini, and onion onto the skewers, alternating between the components.
3. Melt the butter in a small saucepan over low heat, then remove from the heat and mix in the cilantro.
4. Using tongs, grill the skewers for 8 minutes, flipping once and coating with butter, or until the veggies are cooked.

SALAD DE PASTA DE SPAM (WESTERN PASTA SALAD)

INGREDIENTS:
- 12-ounce can SPAM Classic (cut into cubes), drained and rinsed
- 3 cups cooked and drained macaroni and cheese
- 1 cup shredded Cheddar cheese, cubed
- 1 cup shredded carrots
- 3/4 cup celery, finely chopped
- 1/4 cup green bell pepper, finely chopped
- 1/4 cup finely diced onion
- One cup of mayonnaise or salad dressing.
- Creamy mustard blend (about 2 teaspoons)
- barbecue sauce (approximately 1.1/2 tbsp)

INSTRUCTIONS:
1. Add the macaroni, SPAM Classic, cheese, carrots, celery, bell pepper, and onion in a large mixing basin, then toss to blend everything.

2. To prepare the dressing, combine the mayonnaise, mustard, and barbeque sauce in a small mixing bowl until well combined.
3. Toss the macaroni mixture with the dressing until well combined.
4. Refrigerate for 1 hour after covering with plastic wrap.

SPAM SKILLET IN A VARIETY OF COLORS

INGREDIENTS:

- 1 can (12 ounces) of SPAM Cubes with less sodium, split into smaller pieces
- 1 can cream of celery soup (12-ounce can total)
- 1.1/2 quarts of water
- butter or margarine (around a tablespoon)
- 3/4 cup long-grain rice
- 1 box (10 ounces) of frozen peas, defrosted
- Drain 1 jar (4.5-ounces) of sliced mushrooms, rinsed with cold water
- One cup of finely chopped Cheddar cheese is a kind of cheese.

INSTRUCTIONS:

1. Combine the soup, water, and butter in a large pan over medium heat.
2. Bring the mixture to a rolling boil.
3. Combine the SPAM Low in Sodium and the Rice.
4. Continue to cook for another 18 minutes after lowering the heat and covering the pan.
5. Place Rice and mushrooms in a pan and cover with a lid for 15 minutes, or until the Rice is cooked and the peas are heated through thoroughly.
6. Cover the rice mixture with cheese to keep it from drying out. Allow for 5 minutes or until the cheese is completely melted.

PIZZA WITH SPAM FOR BREAKFAST

INGREDIENTS:

- 1 (12-ounce) can SPAM Classic, chopped into cubes, sautéed in a skillet
- 1/4 cup finely chopped onion
- 1/4 cup diced tomato
- 1/4 teaspoon oregano leaves (dried), chopped
- 5 giant eggs (about)
- a quarter cup of milk
- 1/8 teaspoon freshly ground pepper
- 1 (8-ounce) can of crescent roll dough that has been chilled
- half-cup shredded Cheddar cheese, grated
- a quarter cup of sliced ripe olives

INSTRUCTIONS:

1. Preheat the oven to 375 degrees Fahrenheit.
2. Unroll the dough and cut it into triangles to prepare the crust, as shown in the picture.
3. Place the dough triangles in a cast-iron skillet or a 12-inch deep-dish pizza pan with the tips pointing toward the middle of the pan.
4. Press the triangles together to cover the bottom of the pan and 1/2 inch up the sides. Repeat with the remaining triangles.
5. Ten minutes in the oven should be enough.
6. Meanwhile, whisk together the eggs, milk, oregano, and pepper in a large mixing dish.
7. When the 10 minutes are up, gently pour the egg mixture over the crust and spread evenly.
8. Add another 10 minutes to the baking time until the egg mixture is nearly wholly set.
9. Sprinkle the SPAM Classic, tomato, olives, onion, and cheese on top of the egg mixture before serving.

10. Remove from the oven and bake for another 3 to 5 minutes, until the cheese is melted.
11. Cut into wedges and serve immediately.

MINI-QUEUES WITH SPAM AND SPINACH

INGREDIENTS:
- 1 (12-ounce) can SPAM Classic (or similar)
- 8 giant eggs that have been gently beaten
- a half (10-ounce) container of frozen chopped spinach, thawed and pressed to remove moisture
- a half-gallon of milk
- 1/4 cup finely chopped onion
- Swiss cheese (about 1/2 cup shredded)
- half-cup shredded Cheddar cheese, grated
- 1/4 teaspoon freshly grated nutmeg
- 1/8 teaspoon freshly ground pepper
- Refrigerated buttermilk biscuit dough (three 12-ounce cans)

INSTRUCTIONS:
1. Preheat the oven to 350 degrees Fahrenheit.
2. Prepare muffin pans by greasing them.
3. In a large mixing bowl, add the SPAM Classic, the eggs, the spinach, the onion, the milk, the cheeses, the nutmeg, and the pepper, then thoroughly incorporate everything.
4. Place the biscuits in the muffin cups, carefully pushing them into them.
5. Fill each cup halfway with the SPAM filling.
6. Bake quiches for 25 to 30 minutes until the tops are golden brown and the egg mixture is set in the center—warm the dish before serving.

SANDWICH WITH SPAM ON THE BIG ISLAND OF HAWAII

INGREDIENTS:
- 2 slices each of 1 (12-ounce) can of SPAM Classic
- 1-pound can of pineapple rings, drained
- 4-pound hamburger buns, divided and grilled
- 4-pound slice of American cheese

INSTRUCTIONS:
1. Brown the SPAM slices in a pan over medium heat.
2. Two slices of SPAM should be placed on each bottom half of the hamburger bun.
3. Finish with a pineapple ring and a piece of cheese.
4. Top the sandwich with the top half of the bread.

SPAM AND SCRAMBLED EGGS

INGREDIENTS:
- 12-ounce can SPAM Classic (cut into cubes), drained and rinsed
- 1 cup finely chopped fresh chives
- 4 big eggs
- a quarter cup of milk

INSTRUCTIONS:
1. In a mixing bowl, whisk the eggs and milk until well combined.
2. Cook the egg mixture in an oiled pan over medium-high heat, pulling it with a spatula to let the liquid touch the skillet surface until it reaches the desired doneness.

3. Reduce the heat to low and carefully whisk the mixture until the SPAM Classic is well cooked. Remove the pan from the heat and set it aside. Garnish with chives if desired.

SLIDERS WITH KC BBQ SPAM

INGREDIENTS:

- REAL HORMEL Bacon Barbeque Rub on 1 (12-ounce) can of SPAM
- shallots that have been crisped
- Provolone cheese, thinly sliced
- Sauce for barbecuing
- Hawaiian sweet rolls are a dessert that originated in Hawaii.

RUB FOR THE BARBECUE:

- paprika (about 2 tablespoons)
- a third cup of brown sugar
- 2-tablespoons coarse kosher salt
- 1/2 teaspoon freshly ground black pepper

CRISPY SHALLOTS:

- One big or 2 little shallots (depending on size).
- 1 tablespoon of all-purpose flour
- a half teaspoon of salt
- a half teaspoon of paprika
- 1/4 teaspoon freshly ground pepper
- Vegetable or coconut oil is recommended.

INSTRUCTIONS:

1. Cut the shallots into thin slices and put them in a ziplock bag with the remaining ingredients.

2. Add the flour, 1/2 teaspoon of paprika, 1/2 teaspoon of salt, and 1/4 teaspoon of pepper to the bag with the shallots, close the bag, and toss until the shallots are well coated.
3. Heat a small saucepan over medium heat, adding just enough oil to cover the bottom of the pan by 1/4 inch.
4. You may check the temperature of the oil by dropping one shallot piece into it. If the shallot sizzles and becomes golden, the oil is ready.
5. Set all of the shallot pieces in the heated oil and fry until they are golden brown, just a few minutes; then, take them from the oil and place them on a paper towel to cool. Repeat with the remaining shallot pieces.
6. In a small mixing bowl, combine 2 teaspoons paprika, 1/3 cup brown sugar, 2 teaspoons coarse kosher salt, and 1/2 teaspoon black pepper to make the barbecue rub.
7. Half-inch-thick SPAM slices with Real HORMEL Bacon are cut into 1/2-inch pieces and sprinkled with the barbecue seasoning.
8. Using a hot pan coated with nonstick frying spray, fry the SPAM and Real HORMEL Bacon slices until somewhat crispy, for just a few minutes, then turn and repeat. Add a piece of provolone cheese to the pan and let it melt on top for about a minute before removing it from the heat. Remove the pan from the heat.
9. Barbeque sauce should be slathered on the bottom of your bun, followed by cheese-topped SPAM with Real HORMEL Bacon, and crispy shallots on top of the cheese, followed by the bun.

CHEESEBALLS MADE WITH SPAM

INGREDIENTS:
- 1 (12-ounce) can SPAM Classic (or similar)
- 2 cups shredded Cheddar cheese (eight-ounce cup)
- 1 (3-ounce) package of cream cheese that has been softened
- 1/2 teaspoon crumbled dehydrated onion flakes
- 1/2 teaspoon dehydrated onion flakes

- 1/2 teaspoon Worcestershire sauce is a condiment.
- 1/8 teaspoon dijon mustard, ground
- 1/8 teaspoon ground chili pepper
- 3 tablespoons finely chopped fresh parsley
- 1 box crackers
- 2 tablespoons paprika, if desired

INSTRUCTIONS:

1. Finely mince the SPAM Classic in a food processor until it is crumbly.
2. Add the SPAM Classic, shredded cheese, cream cheese, onion flakes, Worcestershire sauce, mustard, and chili powder in a medium-sized mixing bowl, stirring well to include all ingredients.
3. Refrigerate for 1 hour until the mixture is firm to the touch.
4. Form the cheese mixture into a ball and wrap it in wax paper; place it in the refrigerator until ready to serve.
5. When you're ready to serve the cheeseball, roll it in parsley and paprika to coat it. Stack the crackers on a serving platter and serve immediately.

SPAM BREAKFAST BAKE

INGREDIENTS:

- 1 (12-ounce) can SPAM Hickory Smoke, cut into cubes
- 1 (12-ounce) can of smoked salmon
- 2 teaspoons of melted butter
- cream of mushroom soup (one 10-ounce can; 10.75-ounce can)
- 1/2 cup finely diced onion
- Thawed frozen chopped potatoes (about 3 cups total)
- 1/4 cup Italian herbs were cooking cream.
- The 3-tablespoon mixture of ranch seasoning
- refrigerated buttermilk biscuit dough (one 16-ounce can)

- 2 cups of finely shredded sharp Cheddar cheese
- 1 cup sour cream

INSTRUCTIONS:
1. Preheat the oven to 350 degrees Fahrenheit.
2. Prepare a 13-by-nine-inch baking dish with cooking spray.
3. Melt the butter in a large pan over medium-high heat until it begins to foam.
4. Cook, turning regularly, for 10 minutes, or until the onion is golden brown, using SPAM Hickory Smoke as a flavoring.
5. In a large mixing bowl, combine the potatoes, sour cream, ranch seasoning, Soup, cheese, and cooking cream until everything is well combined.
6. Stir in the SPAM mixture until everything is well-combined.
7. Fill the baking dish halfway with the mixture.
8. To assemble, slice each biscuit into six wedges and arrange each wedge on top of the SPAM mixture, with the points pointing upward.
9. Thirty minutes, or until biscuits are cooked through and golden brown, depending on how big your biscuits are.

WAFFLES FILLED WITH SPAM AND CHEESE

INGREDIENTS:
- Spam classic 12 ounces mild
- 1 (12-ounce) can SPAM traditional Cheddar cheese
- a total of 16 eggs
- a half-gallon of buttermilk
- 4 pounds of all-purpose flour (for baking)
- 2 tbsp baking soda
- Baking powder (four tablespoons)
- salt and sugar (a tbsp of each)

- 1-pound melted butter

INSTRUCTIONS:
1. In a mixing basin, whisk the eggs and buttermilk until well combined.
2. Dry waffle batter components should be mixed separately from the wet ingredients.
3. Pour the wet egg and buttermilk mixture into the bowl.
4. Gently combine the ingredients until they are lumpy, then fold in the melted butter until well combined.
5. Using a box grater, shred the SPAM Classic and the cheese.
6. To create Belgian waffles, preheat a cast iron waffle maker to 350°F and pour in 6 ounces of the waffle batter once it is hot.
7. Two ounces of cheddar should be sprinkled on the cheese, followed by 2 ounces of shredded SPAM Classic.
8. Cook the waffle until it is golden and crispy on the outside.

SLIDERS MADE WITH SPICY SPAM

INGREDIENTS:

TO MAKE SAUCE:

- Mayonnaise or salad dressing (around 1 cup)
- 1.1/2 teaspoons spicy sauce
- 1 tsp. paprika, to taste

IN THE CASE OF SLIDERS:

- 12-ounce can of SPAM Classic Vegetable oil for frying 1 quart of water
- 3 giant eggs that have been gently beaten
- 2 cups bread crumbs seasoned with Italian herbs and spices
- a total of 8 slices of cooked bacon, half-cut
- sliced into quarters 4 pineapple rings (fresh or frozen)

INSTRUCTIONS:

1. To make the sauce, put the mayonnaise or salad dressing, spicy sauce, and paprika in a mixing dish and keep away until needed.
2. Heat the oil over medium-high heat (about 375°F) for the sliders.
3. Cut the SPAM Classic into 2-inch pieces (1/4-inch thick) using a sharp knife.
4. Repeat the process with the remaining sliced SPAM Classic, dipping each piece into the egg and then the bread crumbs.
5. Sauté each piece in the oil until golden brown on both sides, then drain well on paper towels to remove excess fat.
6. Combine one slice of SPAM Classic, bacon, pineapple, some barbecue sauce, and the second piece of SPAM Classic in each slider.
7. Using a toothpick, take each slider apart and enjoy! This recipe makes 8 sliders.

MUSUBI TACOS WITH CAULIFLOWER RICE AND SPAM

INGREDIENTS:

- giant dice from one (12-ounce) can of SPAM Classic
- 1 quail (egg)
- 1 cup of all-purpose flour
- 1 cup of iced water
- 3 cups extra-virgin olive oil
- 8 sheets nori, cut into a circular form with scissors
- 1 teaspoon sesame seeds
- 3 cups steamed cauliflower
- a half cup of water
- 2 teaspoons rice vinegar.
- cucumbers, julienned (about 3/4 cup)
- carrots, grated (about 3/4 cup)

- Wasabi
- Soy sauce is a condiment.
- pickled ginger

INSTRUCTIONS:
1. In a medium-sized mixing basin, whisk together the egg.
2. Add the flour and cold water, stirring until the ingredients are well combined.
3. Heat the oil in a big saucepan until it reaches 375°F.
4. One side of a nori sheet should be dipped in the butter mixture.
5. Prepare by carefully frying the nori sheet in heated oil, batter first, for 1 to 2 minutes before turning over and frying on the other side until crisp and curled.
6. Remove the nori from the oil and place it on a sheet pan lined with paper towels, shaping it into a taco shell as it cools.
7. Make 8 taco shells by repeating the process.
8. Cook the diced SPAM Classic over medium-high heat for 3 to 5 minutes, or until it is browned, in a large pan until it is browned.
9. Sesame seeds may be sprinkled on top.
10. Cover the cauliflower in a separate big pan with water and cook over medium heat for 4 to 6 minutes, or until it is tender. Rice vinegar is used to season the dish.
11. Divide the cauliflower rice and SPAM Classic evenly among the nori shells and serve immediately.
12. Cucumbers and carrots are placed on top of the tacos. Toss with wasabi, soy sauce, and pickled ginger before serving.

FRENCH TOAST STICKS WITH SPAM

INGREDIENTS:
- 1 (12-ounce) can SPAM Classic, grated
- 6 giant eggs (about)
- 2 cups shredded Cheddar cheese (eight-ounce cup)
- vanilla essence (around a tablespoon)

- Remove the crusts from 6 pieces of white bread.

INSTRUCTIONS:
1. Combine the SPAM Classic and the cheese in a mixing bowl until thoroughly combined.
2. Whisk together the eggs and vanilla extract in a separate dish until well combined.
3. Each slice of bread should be flattened with a rolling pin on a clean working area.
4. Sprinkle the SPAM mixture over the top of the bread, then roll up the bread and gently press the sides together to secure them in place.
5. Each breadstick should be dipped into the egg mixture and gently turned to cover both sides.
6. Place each breadstick on a pan or skillet that has been lightly coated with nonstick cooking spray and cook over medium heat, flipping gently, until both sides are lightly browned, and the sticks are well warmed.
7. Place the cookies on a platter and gently coat them with powdered sugar and cinnamon to finish them. Pour honey or your preferred syrup over the top to serve as a dipping sauce.

PASTA WITH SPAM

INGREDIENTS:
- 1 can (12 ounces) of SPAM Cut into cubes and browned with less sodium.
- cooked and drained bowtie pasta from a half (16-ounce) package
- freshly picked asparagus stalks, sliced into 1-inch pieces, softly steamed
- half-cup shredded Parmesan cheese, grated
- Alfredo sauce made with sun-dried tomatoes, one (16-ounce) jar

INSTRUCTIONS:
1. Combine the bowtie spaghetti, Alfredo sauce, and SPAM Less Sodium; heat until well cooked.
2. Toss in the asparagus with care.
3. Distribute the SPAM mixture over four dinner plates and top with the cheese.

BREAKFAST ENCHILADAS WITH SPAM CASSEROLE

INGREDIENTS:
- 12-ounce can SPAM Classic (cut into cubes), drained and rinsed
- 1/2 cup green bell pepper, chopped
- 1/2 cup onion, chopped
- 8 fajita-size flour tortillas
- 1/2 cup green bell pepper, chopped
- 1 jar CHI-CHI'S Diced Green Chillies (chili peppers)
- 4 big quail eggs
- 1.5 quarts of shredded Cheddar cheese, split
- 1 tomato, diced
- 2 quarts of heavy whipped cream

INSTRUCTIONS:
1. Place about 1/4 cup of the SPAM Classic cubes in the middle of each tortilla, along with 1 tablespoon of onion, 1 tablespoon of bell pepper, 1 tablespoon of tomato, and 1 tablespoon of cheese. Repeat for each tortilla.
2. Each tortilla should be carefully rolled.

3. Place the tortilla rolls in a greased 13-by-9-inch baking dish and bake for 15 minutes.
4. In a large mixing bowl, whisk together the eggs, cream, and chiles until well combined. Pour the mixture over the enchiladas.
5. Refrigerate the enchiladas overnight to allow the flavors to blend.
6. Preheat the oven to 350 degrees Fahrenheit when you're ready.
7. Bake the casserole for 40 to 50 minutes, or until the egg mixture, is set, and then top with the remaining 1 cup of cheese before serving.
8. Bake for another 5 minutes, or until the cheese is melted. Serve with Picante sauce on the side.

WHEN PIGS FLY, SPAM BITES

INGREDIENTS:
- 1 can (12 ounces) of SPAM Grated hot and spicy peppers
- 1 packet of boil-in-bag vegetables Rice with jasmine fragrance
- 3 quail eggs
- Mexican mix cheese, shredded 1 cup
- One cup of finely shredded sharp cheese Cheddar cheese is a kind of cheese.
- 1 tablespoon chives (dry), chopped
- 2 tbsp. Freshly chopped parsley.
- Using cooking spray
- 1.1/2 cup panko bread crumbs
- 3/4 cup pecans that have been finely chopped
- Combine 2 tablespoons Cajun seasoning with 1 cup Ranch and Blue Cheese salad dressing for dipping.

INSTRUCTIONS:
1. Preheat the oven to 375 degrees Fahrenheit.

2. Prepare the Rice according to the package instructions, then drain and put aside the Rice.
3. In a large nonstick pan, heat the shredded SPAM Hot and Spicy and the chives over medium heat until the SPAM is gently browned. Remove from the heat and leave aside to cool somewhat.
4. Rice and SPAM Hot & Spicy should be put in a mixing basin before adding the shredded cheeses and 1 egg. Mix until the mixture is fully incorporated.
5. Form the SPAM mixture into little bite-sized balls and set them on a baking sheet lined with parchment paper. Repeat with the remaining SPAM mixture.
6. In a separate dish, whisk the egg whites until they are foamy.
7. Mix the bread crumbs, pecans, parsley, and Cajun seasoning in a separate bowl until well combined.
8. Each SPAM ball should be dipped into the egg whites and then coated with the breadcrumb mixture before returning them to the baking pan with parchment paper.
9. Bake for 15 minutes at 375°F, or until the top is gently browned.
10. Prepare the meatballs by inserting a toothpick in the middle of each one and serving with ranch and blue cheese salad dressings on the side for dipping. This recipe makes 24 servings.

WONTONS FILLED WITH SPAM

INGREDIENTS:
- 1 can (seven-ounce) SPAM Classic, diced
- 1 cup chicken broth
- 1 clove of chopped garlic
- 1 cup water
- 1 tablespoon of ice-cold water
- 1 tablespoon cornstarch
- 1 tablespoon finely chopped fresh cilantro
- 1 cup finely chopped onion

- 16 cilantro leaves (fresh or dried)
- 1 cup red potato coarsely chopped
- a quarter teaspoon of ground allspice
- a quarter teaspoon of ground cumin
- 1/4 teaspoon freshly ground pepper
- 1/4 teaspoon freshly ground salt
- a total of 36 wonton wrappers

INSTRUCTIONS:

1. Preheat the oven to 400 degrees Fahrenheit.
2. Heat two baking sheets in the oven for 10 minutes or until they are hot.
3. Meanwhile, put the first 10 ingredients in a pot and set them aside.
4. Bring the mixture to a boil over medium heat, stirring regularly. Remove from heat and set aside.
5. Once the water is boiling, decrease the heat to low and cook for 8 minutes, stirring periodically, or until the potato is cooked.
6. Remove from heat and set aside to cool.
7. To drain the SPAM mixture, set a colander over a large mixing basin and pour the mixture into the strainer. Remove the liquid from the container.
8. Cut the SPAM mixture into small pieces with a knife, or pulse it twice or thrice in a food processor until it is finely minced.
9. Whisk together the cornstarch and cold water in a large mixing basin until smooth.
10. Spoon 1 spoonful of the SPAM mixture into the middle of each wonton wrapper, one at a time, working with 1 wonton wrapper at a time (Cover remaining wrappers with a damp towel to keep them moist).
11. The cornstarch mixture should be used to moisten the edges of the wrappers. Bring the opposing corners together and squeeze the tips together to seal them, forming triangles.
12. Using a cooking spray, coat the baking sheets once they have been removed from the oven.

13. Using a single layer of wonton wrappers, arrange the filled wonton wrappers on baking sheets and spray the wonton wrappers with cooking spray.
14. Bake for 8 minutes, rotating halfway through, or until golden brown. Garnish with cilantro if desired.

HAWAIIAN PIZZA WITH SPAM

INGREDIENTS:
- sliced into thin squares 1 (12-ounce) can SPAM Classic (Classic)
- 1 (10-ounce) can of pre-made pizza crust that has been chilled
- 1 (6-ounce) box of sliced Provolone cheese (or similar cheese).
- 12 ounces chunked pineapple (drained)
- 16-ounce can of pineapple chunks
- a half cup of finely chopped red onion
- 1/2 cup finely sliced green pepper

INSTRUCTIONS:
1. Preheat the oven to 425 degrees Fahrenheit.
2. Prepare a 14-inch pizza pan or a 13-by-39-inch baking pan with cooking spray.
3. Unroll the dough and push it into the pan that has been prepared.
4. Finish with a sprinkling of cheese.
5. Place the remaining ingredients on top of the cheese.
6. Thirty minutes, or until the crust is a deep golden brown, should be enough time to bake it.

CASSEROLE OF TATER TOTS WITH SPAM

INGREDIENTS:

- 1 can SPAM with Real HORMEL Bacon Cut into 1/4-inch cubes
- 1 bag frozen tater tots
- 12 eggs, beaten
- 3 cups shredded sharp cheddar cheese
- 1 small yellow onion, peeled and chopped
- 1 teaspoon hot and spicy smoked paprika
- 1 tablespoon onion powder
- 1 tablespoon of salt
- 1 teaspoon of black pepper

INSTRUCTIONS:

1. Using butter, sauté the onions until tender, then remove them from the pan and place them on a baking sheet to cool.
2. Fry the SPAM cubes until they are crisp and golden brown in the same pan.
3. Return the sautéed onions to the frying pan and remove the pan from the heat.
4. Separately, in a large mixing bowl, whisk together the eggs, cheese, paprika, onion powder, salt, and plenty of black pepper until well combined. Set aside.
5. Then, combine the tater tots with the sautéed onion and SPAM mixture in a large mixing bowl before transferring the mixture to a baking tray.
6. 350°F for 45 minutes, then broil for 15-20 minutes more until the top is golden brown and the sides are crisp.

SPAMALICIOUS FIESTA DIP

INGREDIENTS:

- 12-ounce can of SPAM Jalapeno flavored SPAM
- 10-ounce can of chopped tomatoes with green chiles (or similar).
- a total of two (8-ounce) containers of cream cheese
- a half-cup of sour cream

- Toss together 1 (15-ounce) can of corn, and drained Tortilla chips (for dipping), and serve.

INSTRUCTIONS:

1. Cook the SPAM Jalapeno in a 3-quart pot until it is gently browned, about 3 minutes.
2. Combine the chopped tomatoes, green chilies, sour cream, and corn in a large mixing bowl. The dip should be warm after the Ingredients are thoroughly blended and the cream cheese has melted.
3. Serve with tortilla chips for dipping as an accompaniment. This recipe serves 16-20 people.

JACK, SPAM, AND OTHERS

INGREDIENTS:

- 1 (12-ounce) can SPAM Classic, cut into small pieces 1/8 inch in thickness (4 slices)
- a pound and a half Camembert (Monterey Jack cheese)
- 4 tablespoons of giardiniera, coarsely chopped
- 4 tablespoons beer mustard
- Pretzel bread is sliced into loaves (8 slices)
- 2-4 teaspoons of melted butter

INSTRUCTIONS:
1. Cook the SPAM Classic until it is crispy and browned on both sides, about 10 minutes total.
2. Pretzel bread may be used to make a sandwich. Cheese, chopped giardiniera, and mustard are sprinkled on top.
3. Grill or toast the sandwich on medium heat in a skillet with melted butter until the cheese is melted and the toasting of the sandwich is complete.

SANDWICH WITH SPAM IN THE STYLE OF THE MONTE CRISTO

INGREDIENTS:
- 1 (12-ounce) can SPAM Classic (or similar)
- 3 teaspoons of melted butter
- 2 giant eggs (about)
- a quarter cup of milk
- Sliced 6 slices of Muenster cheese and 12 slices of white bread into quarters

INSTRUCTIONS:
1. Cook the SPAM Classic until it is golden brown, cutting it into 12 pieces.
2. Six pieces of bread are layered with cheese and SPAM Classic, and the remaining slices of bread are covered with the remaining portions.
3. In a large mixing bowl, whisk together the eggs and milk. Quickly dip both sides of the sandwiches into the egg mixture to coat them.
4. Sauté the sandwiches in margarine on a grill or in a pan over medium heat until the cheese is melted and both sides are browned.

SPAM MONKEY BREAD

INGREDIENTS:

- Spam with real HORMEL Bacon in a 12-ounce can
- 2 (16.3 ounces) cans butter flavored biscuits from the refrigerator
- 1/2 cup sugar (about)
- 1 tsp. ground cinnamon
- 3/4 cup melted butter
- honey (about 2 teaspoons)
- 1 cup granulated sugar
- 2 1/2 teaspoons bourbon with a maple flavoring
- Tube pan with a diameter of ten inches
- Using cooking spray

INSTRUCTIONS:

1. Preheat the oven to 350 degrees Fahrenheit.
2. Cooking spray should be used to oil a 10-inch fluted tube pan thoroughly.
3. 1/4-inch cubes of the SPAM product should be used.
4. Cook the SPAM cubes in a pan over medium heat until crisp, about 5 minutes. Transfer it to a dish lined with a paper towel to allow it to cool.
5. In the meanwhile, cut each biscuit into eight equal pieces.
6. In a big zip-top plastic bag, combine the sugar and cinnamon.
7. Small batches of biscuit pieces should be added at a time. Seal the bag after each set and shake vigorously until the components are equally covered.
8. In a shallow baking pan, layer 1/3 of the chopped SPAM product.
9. Half of the sugared biscuit pieces should be placed on top, followed by another third of the SPAM product.
10. Set aside the leftover biscuit pieces and the remaining SPAM product when you finish assembling them.
11. Over medium heat, melt the butter in a small saucepan, constantly stirring, until the butter is browned (approximately 5 minutes).

12. Whisk in the brown sugar, honey, and bourbon until smooth, then pour over the biscuits in an equal layer over the top.
13. Bake for 30-35 minutes until the biscuits are golden brown and the filling has been set. Allow the bread to cool for a few minutes before flipping it onto a baking sheet or tray and serving it immediately.

SPAM LAZY DAY CASSEROLE

INGREDIENTS:
- sliced into strips (12-ounce) can SPAM Classic
- 8 ounces of medium egg noodles
- 1 box (10.75-ounces) of frozen spinach
- 1 package (10.75-ounces) of frozen spinach
- Two tablespoons of butter or margarine.
- 2 tbsp. all-purpose flour
- 1 and a third cups milk
- 1 cup sour cream
- 1/2 teaspoon of salt
- for one 10-ounce box of frozen peas, thawed
- 1 package of frozen corn
- 4 pinches paprika
- pepper, according to personal preference

INSTRUCTIONS:
1. Preheat the oven to 375 degrees Fahrenheit.
2. Prepare a 13-by-9-inch baking dish by lightly greasing it.
3. Cook the spinach according to the package instructions and drain well.
4. Spread spinach over the bottom of the baking dish to provide a bed for the chicken.
5. Cook the egg noodles according to the package instructions before draining.
6. Meanwhile, stir the butter in a medium saucepan over medium heat until creamy.

7. Continue to simmer and stir the mixture over medium heat, constantly stirring, until it thickens and begins to boil.
8. A tiny portion of the hot milk mixture should be mixed into the sour cream before adding it to the pot.
9. Combine the SPAM Classic with the peas.
10. Combine the white sauce and noodles in a large mixing bowl, then pour over the spinach and sprinkle with paprika.
11. Cover with aluminum foil and bake for 20 minutes.
12. Remove the lid and bake for another 20 minutes.

BITES OF SPAM ENCASED WITH BACON

INGREDIENTS:
- 32 cubes of SPAM Classic from a 12-ounce can
- applesauce (about 2 tablespoons)
- 1/2 cup honey mustard
- 1 packet HORMEL BLACK LABEL Bacon (about 1 pound)
- 1/4 cup brown sugar that has been packed

INSTRUCTIONS:
1. Preheat the oven to 400 degrees Fahrenheit.
2. Cook the bacon until partially cooked and drain on a paper towel. Each piece of bacon should be cut in half.
3. Wrap the bacon around each cube of SPAM Classic and attach it with a wooden toothpick to create a sandwich.
4. Place the SPAM bits in a 13x9-inch baking tray and bake for 15 minutes.
5. Combine the mustard, brown sugar, and apple juice in a mixing bowl until thoroughly combined.
6. Drizzle the mustard mixture over the SPAM Classic wrapped in bacon.
7. Bake for 15 to 20 minutes until the bacon is crisp and golden.

APPETIZER WITH SPAM (ISLAND STYLE)

INGREDIENTS:

- 2 crescent roll dough cans (8 ounces each) from the refrigerator
- 1 can (12 ounces) of SPAM Traditionally prepared, finely chopped
- 2 crescent roll dough cans (8 ounces each) from the refrigerator
- 1 (8-ounce) box of cream cheese that has been beaten
- 2/3 cup mayonnaise
- 1/2 (8-ounce) can of crushed pineapple that has been drained thoroughly 1 lime zest
- 2 bunches of finely sliced green onions
- Drain and rinse one 15-ounce can of black beans before using.
- 1 red bell pepper, seeded and diced (about 1 tablespoon) (2.25-ounce) sliced ripe olives in a jar
- 2 tablespoons extra-virgin olive oil
- 2 tbsp lime juice
- 1 garlic clove, peeled and minced
- a quarter teaspoon of salt
- a quarter teaspoon of ground cumin
- a quarter teaspoon of red pepper flakes, crushed
- 1/8 teaspoon freshly ground white pepper
- 1-2 tablespoons finely chopped Blend of jerk seasonings
- cheese (about 1 cup shredded cheddar)

INSTRUCTIONS:

1. In a large mixing bowl, add 1 bunch of green onions, the black beans, the red bell pepper, the olives, the olive oil, the lime juice, the garlic, the salt, the ground cumin, the crushed red pepper flakes, and the freshly ground white pepper.
2. Refrigerate for several hours or overnight after covering the bowl.

3. To make the dressing, combine the cream cheese, mayonnaise, crushed pineapple, 4 sliced green onions, and the zest of 1 lime in another large mixing bowl.
4. Cover the bowl with plastic wrap and place it in the refrigerator until ready to use it.
5. Preheat the oven to 400 degrees Fahrenheit.
6. Place the unrolled crescent roll dough into a jellyroll pan 10 to 15 inches in diameter.
7. Remove from the oven and set aside to cool for 10 minutes or until the top is golden brown.
8. In a large pan, cook the SPAM Classic with the Jerk spice until crisp and golden brown, then remove from heat and set aside.
9. When it's ready to serve, spread the cream cheese filling on top of the crust, followed by the black bean salsa, the sautéed SPAM Classic, and the cheese.
10. Cut into squares or triangles and place on a plate to serve.

SOUP WITH SPAM AND GNOCCHI

INGREDIENTS:
- 1 (12-ounce) can SPAM Classic (or similar)
- 1 tablespoon extra-virgin olive oil
- 1 small onion, peeled and chopped
- 3 celery stalks, peeled and chopped
- 3 garlic cloves, peeled and minced
- peeled and shredded carrots (two carrots)
- 4 quarts of homemade chicken broth
- 1 box small potato gnocchi (about 16 ounces)
- Baby spinach greens (about a six-ounce package)
- 1 tablespoon cornstarch
- 1/2 cup heavy cream
- 1 teaspoon salt
- 2 teaspoons cold water
- 2 cups half-and-half cream
- 1 teaspoon freshly ground pepper

INSTRUCTIONS:

1. *In a large saucepan, boil the olive oil over medium heat until shimmering. In a large mixing bowl, combine the onion, celery, garlic, and carrots—Cook for approximately 5 minutes until the onion is transparent.*
2. *Bring the SPAM and chicken broth to a boil while stirring constantly.*
3. *Cook the gnocchi in the boiling broth for 3 to 4 minutes, or until they begin to float to the top of the pot. Toss in the spinach and simmer for approximately 3 minutes, or until it has wilted.*
4. *Whisk the cornstarch and cold water together in a small mixing basin until smooth. Pour the cornstarch and half-and-half into the boiling soup and stir until smooth.*
5. *Cook for approximately 5 minutes, or until the Soup thickens somewhat—season with salt and freshly ground pepper.*

MUSUBI WITH BBQ SPAM

INGREDIENTS:

- *2 teaspoons extra-virgin olive oil*
- *2 slices each of 1 (12-ounce) can of SPAM Classic*
- *1 tablespoon of distilled water*
- *a half cup of barbecue sauce*
- *3 cups sushi rice that has been cooked*
- *4 nori sheets, each half-sheeted*

INSTRUCTIONS:

1. *Heat the oil in a large skillet over medium-high heat until shimmering—Cook SPAM Classic for 2 to 3 minutes, or until it begins to brown. Combine the water and BBQ sauce in a large mixing bowl—Cook for 2 to 3 minutes, or until the sauce has reduced and has a glaze consistency.*

2. Insert nori sheet halves into the center of the musubi press or plastic-lined SPAM Classic can and press down. Repeat with remaining Rice until all of the nori sheet halves are used. Finish with a piece of SPAM Classic. Take away the press.
3. Wrap each nori sheet in a single layer. To attach the two ends, moisten one end gently with water. Make another eight by repeating the process.

EAST MEETS WEST IN THE FORM OF SPAM ROLLS

INGREDIENTS:
- 1 can (12 ounces) of SPAM Sodium-reduced, diced
- 1 box egg roll wrappers (about)
- 1/2 gallon of sauerkraut, drained and pressed
- 2 cups shredded Gruyère cheese
- 1/4 cup Thousand Island dressing.
- A quarter cup of water

INSTRUCTIONS:
1. Fill a small dipping dish or cup halfway with water.
2. To make the egg roll wrappers, place a generous spoonful of dressing in the middle of each wrapper, leaving approximately 1 inch on each side.
3. One tablespoon of SPAM Less Sodium may be sprinkled on top of the dressing.
4. One tablespoon of sauerkraut should be spread over the SPAM.
5. One tablespoon of cheese should be sprinkled on top.
6. To help seal the edges, dip your fingers into the water and distribute the water evenly around the edges.
7. Fold the left edge over approximately 1/2 inch to overlap the right side of the frame. Repeat the process on the other side.
8. Bring the bottom of the container up over the filling.

9. Roll the wrapper up into an egg roll shape, sliding your finger over the seam to seal the roll together.
10. Invert them onto their backs with the seam side down and press hard on the left and right sides, ensuring that the roll is completely closed.
11. Heat the oil to 375 degrees Fahrenheit in a large, heavy skillet. Fry approximately 4 egg rolls at a time, rotating them every minute, for 2 to 3 minutes, or until they are golden brown on both sides (about 2 to 3 minutes total). Transfer to a wire rack on a sheet pan to allow the excess liquid to drain.
12. If preferred, SPAM rolls should be served warm, with spicy brown or sweet hot mustard on the side.

JUICY LUCY SPAM BURGER HAMBURGER

INGREDIENTS:
- classic SPAM (two slices)
- 1 toasted potato slider bread
- 2 ounces Cheddar slices
- 1-pound ground beef

INSTRUCTIONS:
1. Heat the SPAM Classic according to the package instructions until golden brown.
2. One SPAM Classic slice should be topped with cheese slices and the remaining SPAM Classic slice.
3. Assemble the burger by layering it with SPAM Classic and cheese, then topping it with your favorite ingredients.

BREAKFAST MUFFINS WITH SPAMKINS

INGREDIENTS:

- 1 (12-ounce) can SPAM with REAL HORMEL. Cubed bacon, sautéed in a tiny quantity of butter until crispy
- 1.1/2 cups all-purpose flour (about)
- 1/4 cup melted butter (approximately)
- 1 teaspoon of cinnamon, ground
- 4 giant eggs, cut in half
- 1/3 cup maple syrup with a hint of maple taste
- two and quarter-ounce packages of rapid-rise yeast are a kind of yeast that proliferates.
- a half teaspoon of salt
- Divide 2 teaspoons of sugar with 1/2 cup of water.
- 2/3 cup warm milk plus 2 teaspoons warm cream (distributed)

INSTRUCTIONS:

1. Cooking spray should be used to coat 18 regular-size muffin cups lightly.
2. Mix all ingredients in a large mixing basin until thoroughly combined. Add the yeast, 2 tbsp sugar, salt, 2/3 cup milk, the butter, and 1 egg and mix well.
3. Fill each muffin cup halfway with batter (approximately 1 tablespoon per muffin cup).
4. The remaining 1/2 cup sugar and the cinnamon should be combined in a small mixing dish; stir thoroughly.
5. Divide the sugar-cinnamon mixture in half and sprinkle it over the muffins.
6. Over each muffin, sprinkle approximately 1 tbsp SPAM with Real HORMEL Bacon (about 1 tablespoon total).
7. Separately, mix the remaining 3 eggs and 2 tablespoons of milk in a separate dish until well combined.
8. Pour roughly 1 spoonful of the egg mixture over each muffin and top with a drizzle of maple syrup to finish.
9. Place the muffin pans in a cold oven and preheat the oven to 350 degrees Fahrenheit.
10. The muffins should be baked for 15 to 20 minutes, or until the egg mixture is set, once your oven has reached the proper temperature.

11. Remove the muffin tins from the oven and allow them to cool in the pan for 5 minutes before removing them.
12. Removing the muffins from the pan and serving them warm or at room temperature is an option. If desired, drizzle with extra maple syrup for dipping sauce.

SPAM RED FLANNEL HASH

INGREDIENTS:
- chopped from 1 (12-ounce) can of SPAM Classic
- 16-ounce can-eat beets, drained and chopped
- 1 medium onion, finely chopped
- 1-pound of diced potatoes, cooked from 4 medium potatoes
- 2 tbsp. vegetable oil

INSTRUCTIONS:
1. In a large pan, sauté the onion in the oil, turning regularly, until it is lightly browned, about 10 minutes.
2. Cook for 5 minutes, often stirring, until the SPAM Classic and potatoes are heated.
3. Season with pepper and stir in the beets until well combined.
4. Cook for 10 minutes after covering with a lid and turning the heat low.
5. Cook for another 5 minutes after removing the lid.

SPAMLT OG SLIDER

INGREDIENTS:
- One 12-ounce can of SPAM Classic, sliced into nine slices

- 1 (12-ounce) package of Hawaiian sweet rolls, divided and gently toasted
- thinly sliced medium yellow onion, caramelized
- 1 medium yellow onion, caramelized
- 2 Roma tomatoes, thinly sliced into 12 portions
- butter lettuce (about 1 cup finely shredded)
- 1/2 cup snow peas or watercress, thinly sliced
- 12 tablespoons Volcanic Aioli (Vulcanic Sauce) (recipe below)

INSTRUCTIONS:

1. The Volcanic Aioli may be made by combining 1/2 cup mayonnaise, 1.1/2 teaspoons Sriracha hot chili sauce, 1/4 teaspoon garlic chili paste, and 1/8 teaspoon sesame oil in a separate bowl. Make a mental note to put it away.
2. For the Sliders, cut each slice of SPAM Classic in half and fry in a pan until browned on both sides, about 5 minutes total time.
3. To finish, spread a small amount of Volcanic Aioli over the bottom half of each bun and arrange a few caramelized onions on top of the sauce to look like snow.
4. Add 1.1/2 slices of SPAM Classic, a piece of tomato, some butter lettuce, and snow peas on each roll before rolling it up.
5. Cover with the tops of the rolls and drizzle with more Volcanic Aioli.

SPAM POTATO SALAD

INGREDIENTS:

- 12-ounce can SPAM Classic (cut into cubes), drained and rinsed
- 1/2 cup dill pickles, finely chopped
- cooked carrots, diced (about 1/2 cup)
- 2 tablespoons pickle brine (dill pickle)
- 1/4 cup finely chopped onion
- 1 cup thawed frozen peas (about 1/2 cup)

- 6 to 7 tablespoons of mayonnaise or salad dressing
- 1 teaspoon of dijon mustard
- potatoes weighing 2 lbs (about 6 medium)

INSTRUCTIONS:

1. Cook the potatoes until they are soft in a large saucepan of boiling water, then drain.
2. Allow cooling for a few minutes before peeling. After that, let it cool to room temperature before cutting it into 1/2-inch cubes.
3. Combine the SPAM Classic and the potatoes in a large mixing basin. Toss in the carrots, peas, pickles, and onion until everything is well distributed.
4. Whisk together the mayonnaise, pickle brine, and mustard in a separate dish until well combined. Gently fold the mixture into the SPAM.
5. Cover and place in the refrigerator for several hours before using.

BABY REDS WITH SPAMENTO CHEESE

INGREDIENTS:

- chopped from 1 (12-ounce) can of SPAM Classic
- 1 tablespoon of melted butter
- 1 medium red bell pepper, diced
- 1/2 medium red bell pepper, diced
- 24 tiny red potatoes split in half, with whipped pimento cheese spread
- 1 and a half tablespoons of salt
- 1 teaspoon freshly ground black pepper
- 2 tablespoons extra-virgin olive oil
- 2 tablespoons finely chopped chives to serve as a garnish
- cayenne pepper (half a teaspoon)

INSTRUCTIONS:

1. Preheat the oven to 400 degrees Fahrenheit.
2. Heat the SPAM Classic in a big pan with some butter until it is nicely browned. Drain the water well.
3. Place the pimento cheese spread in a blender, process until smooth, then transfer to a large mixing bowl.
4. Combine the chopped red bell pepper and the SPAM Classic (reserving about 1/3 of the SPAM Classic for garnish).
5. Wash and scrub the potatoes until they are spotless. Using a spoon or a Parisian scoop, cut each potato in half and scoop out the center of each side.
6. Mix the olive oil, salt, and pepper in a small bowl. Make a paste from the potato halves and arrange them on a baking sheet with the sliced side facing up.
7. Preheat the oven to 400°F and bake for approximately 25 minutes, or until the potatoes are tender when poked with a knife.
8. Remove from the oven and spoon the SPAMento cheese mixture into the middle of the pie.
9. Decorate the potatoes with the SPAM Classic that was preserved from the filling, chives, and a sprinkle of cayenne pepper, if preferred. Serve as soon as possible. This recipe makes 48 servings.

BBQ SANDWICH WITH SPAM

INGREDIENTS:

- chopped 1 can (12 ounces) SPAM Classic, finely chopped
- a third cup of barbecue sauce
- 1-pint coleslaw
- 6 hamburger buns or Kaiser rolls that have been divided and lightly toasted

INSTRUCTIONS:

1. Combine the SPAM Hickory Smoke and barbecue sauce in a mixing basin.
2. Flicking the pan repeatedly will ensure that the SPAM mixture is heated through.
3. If desired, distribute the SPAM mixture equally among the buns and top each with a third cup of coleslaw.

SPAMMY TOTS

INGREDIENTS:

IN THE CASE OF THE ONIGIRI:

- prepared sushi rice (cooled and set out to dry in a cold and ventilated location) 4 cups
- 3 tablespoons Furikake (fermented seaweed)
- 1/4 cup rice wine vinegar

TO USE THE POKE:

- 1-pound of sushi-quality fish Ahi tuna is a kind of fish. Consuming raw or undercooked seafood may raise your chances of contracting a foodborne disease.
- 1 teaspoon finely minced garlic and ginger
- 2 teaspoons finely chopped scallions
- Soy sauce (aloha shoyu is preferred): 2-3 teaspoons
- 2-3 teaspoons of kewpie mayo.
- 1 tbl. mirin
- 12 tablespoons sesame oil
- peppercorns, ground white

FOR THE TERIYAKI WITH BLOOD ORANGE:

- 4 blood oranges, divided and tiny diced, drained, with the juice saved for later use
- 1/2 cup freshly squeezed orange juice
- 1/2 cup mirin
- 1-ounce ginger root, peeled and coarsely chopped
- 1 cup granulated sugar
- 1/2 cup tamari (soy sauce)
- 1 tablespoon freshly ground black pepper, coarsely chopped
- 1-2 ounces chicken or duck liver pate for assembly
- One can (12 ounces) of SPAM was Removed from the can and frozen overnight; this is a classic.
- 2 ounces finely minced scallions
- Toasted sesame seeds

INSTRUCTIONS:

1. Working swiftly and thoroughly with moist hands or a mixer, add all ingredients and thoroughly mix them.
2. Form into SPAM musubi molds and press to a thickness of 12" (approximate).
3. Fry the rice patty (onigiri) until gently brown in a fryer filled with oil heated to 375°F. Drain on a piece of paper towel.
4. Combine all the ingredients and taste, adding additional soy sauce if necessary to balance the flavor.
5. Using a small pot, combine all ingredients and reduce until half or nappe is reached. Refrigerate immediately and put away.
6. Using a spoon, scoop a dollop of poke into the rice patty (onigiri) and place it on a platter. Top with sliced pate and drizzle with teriyaki sauce before serving.
7. Serve with sesame seeds and scallions as garnish. Serve.

SPAM

INGREDIENTS:

CAJUN SEASONING:

- Dried oregano, 2 teaspoons
- Dried basil, 2.1/2 teaspoons
- 1-teaspoon thyme leaves dried
- 2 teaspoons black peppercorns (or other similar spices)
- 1/4 cup white pepper
- 1 tablespoon salt
- onions, powdered (2 teaspoons),
- One cup cayenne pepper (about 3 tsp.
- 4 tbsp. smoked paprika (sweet)
- one-fourth cup of spicy paprika, minced
- garlic powder (about two teaspoons)
- Brown sugar (one tablespoon)

THE ROUX'S STRUCTURE:

- Sea salt is a kind of salt found in the ocean or shore.
- Bacon fat (about 12 cups)
- flour (all-purpose) 1 cup (total)
- unsalted butter (about 2 tablespoons)

TO USE IN THE SPAMBO FORMULA

- 1-can of SPAM Classic (12-ounce size)
- finely chopped 1 cup celery (around a cup)
- finely sliced 1 medium-sized onion
- finely sliced 1 big green bell pepper
- olive oil, a dash at a time
- Water (one gallon).
- Beef stock with no additional salt (two 32-ounce containers)
- 12 pounds of sliced andouille sausage
- garlic, minced (about 2 cloves total)
- sugar (white) - 1 tablespoon
- sea salt (around a pinch)
- the equivalent of two teaspoons of hot pepper sauce

- 1 bunch thyme
- 1/2 teaspoon thyme leaves, dried
- Cook 1 can of stewed tomatoes (14 ounces) until soft.
- Tomato sauce in a 6-ounce can
- of file powder (about 2 tablespoons)
- Two packets of frozen, sliced okra (20 ounces package) or 2 pounds of fresh okra (depending on availability).
- vinegar (apple cider vinegar, 2 teaspoons)
- 1-pound lump of blue crab, either freshly collected or from a can
- 3 pounds raw shrimp (about 21-25 total)
- Worcestershire sauce (about 2 teaspoons)
- white Rice that has been cooked (lightly salted)

INSTRUCTIONS:

1. The Cajun seasoning may be made by putting the black peppercorns in a spice grinder, finely grinding them, and then placing them in a medium-sized mixing basin.
2. Add all the other Cajun seasoning components to a spice grinder, including oregano, basil, 1 tablespoon thyme, white pepper, onion powder, cayenne pepper, sweet paprika, hot paprika, garlic powder, and brown sugar. Process until finely ground. Pulse until the ingredients are finely ground.
3. Combine the black peppercorns and Cajun spice in a large mixing bowl until thoroughly combined. Keep the mixture in a clean Mason jar.
4. To create the SPAMBO, Cut the SPAM Classic into 14-inch cubes, then cook the SPAM and andouille sausage in a nonstick pan until the SPAM and andouille sausage are browned. Drain the liquid onto paper towels and put it aside.
5. Bring 1 quart of water and all beef stock to a low boil in a large, heavy-bottomed soup pot until the water is just boiling.
6. Meanwhile, heat a nonstick pan with a drizzle of olive oil over medium heat until hot. Cook the Trinity (or the celery, onion, and bell pepper) in some oil until soft, then season with Cajun spice. Please do not brown. Remove the skillet from the heat and put it aside.
7. In a nonstick skillet, increase the heat beneath the pan.

8. To prepare the roux, heat the bacon drippings and butter in a pan over medium heat until the butter is melted. Gradually incorporate the flour into the melted bacon fat and butter, stirring gently and continuously between each addition. The mixture will bubble and seem to be doing nothing for a short period until it begins to darken. It will first become the color of brown mustard, then baked bread, then pecan shell, and eventually, a deep, rich brown is desired. This might take anywhere from 20 to 30 minutes to occur. Please be patient. Remove the pan from the heat and continue to stir. Your flour continues to cook as a result of the oil.
9. Then, add the SPAM Classic, andouille sausage, and minced garlic to the roux, and cook until the vegetables are soft, about 10 minutes total. Continue to stir.
10. In a small bowl, whisk together the roux and the low-boiling stock. Reduce the heat to a low simmer for 5 minutes.
11. Combine the white sugar, sea salt to taste, and red pepper sauce in a mixing bowl. Stir thoroughly, and then add the Cajun spice blend until the desired flavor is achieved.
12. The bay leaves, 1/2 teaspoon dried thyme, stewed tomatoes, and tomato sauce should all be added. Continue to cook, constantly stirring, for 60 minutes. Add the file powder when the timer reaches 45 minutes.
13. Heat 1/4 cup of bacon drippings and the sliced okra in a pan until the okra is tender. Add 2 tablespoons of apple cider vinegar to the pot to prevent the okra from getting slimy while it cooks, stirring well. Cook for 15-20 minutes at low heat.
14. Cook on low heat for a few minutes, being careful not to burn the bottom of the soup pot, then add the okra and let it boil for a few minutes.
15. Cook white Rice (lightly salted) for 1 hour before serving, then add blue crab, raw shrimp, and Worcestershire sauce to the rice mixture. Continue to cook until the shrimp is done.
16. When you're ready to serve, remove the bay leaves and season with salt, pepper, and spicy sauce to your liking. Place a hearty scoop of fluffy Rice in the middle of a large serving dish to serve your visitors.
17. To add color to the Rice, sprinkle a Cajun spice mix on top.

18. Prepare the dish by slicing crusty French bread, adding spicy sauce, and gently sweetened iced tea.

SPAM WITH RAMEN NOODLES

INGREDIENTS:
- 3 (3-ounce) packets of SPAM Classic
- 1 (12-ounce) can SPAM Classic cubed Soup with ramen noodles and chicken flavoring
- 1 tablespoon extra-virgin olive oil
- 2 cups broccoli florets (cut in half)
- 1/2 cup sliced yellow bell pepper
- 1/2 cup halved cherry tomatoes
- the equivalent of 2 tablespoons of HOUSE OF TSANG dipping sauce with sweet chilies
- Toppings suggested include chopped cilantro, diced jalapenos, and soft-cooked eggs to taste if you like it spicy.

INSTRUCTIONS:
1. Prepare the noodles according to the package instructions, including the spice packet. After draining, discarding the liquid, and putting the noodles aside,
2. Cook SPAM Classic for 2 to 3 minutes in a large pan over medium heat. Remove the skillet from the heat.
3. Continue to cook the broccoli and bell pepper in the same pan over medium heat for 3 to 4 minutes, or until crisp-tender, in the same skillet over medium heat.
4. Toss in the tomatoes, sweet chili sauce, and the saved noodles to cover everything in the sauce.
5. Add in the SPAM Classic and mix well.
6. As desired, garnish with the recommended toppings.

SPAM WITH RAMEN FROM GENERAL TSO'S KITCHEN

INGREDIENTS:
- Matchsticks made from 1/2 (12-ounce) can of SPAM Classic
- 2 packets (3 ounces each) of Noodles with an Oriental flavor
- 1 tablespoon of extra-virgin olive oil
- 1 cup of snow peas
- cut 1 cup of red bell pepper into strips
- 1 cup green bell pepper
- the equivalent of 2 tablespoons of General Tso's stir-fry sauce from the HOUSE OF TSANG

INSTRUCTIONS:
1. Using the instructions on the box, cook the ramen noodles, including the spice packet. After draining, discarding the liquid, and putting the noodles aside,
2. Heat the oil over medium-high heat in a large pan and cook the SPAM Classic for 2 to 3 minutes, stirring occasionally.
3. Cook for 2 minutes after adding the snow peas and red bell pepper.
4. Toss in the General Tso's sauce and the saved noodles to cover everything.

NACHOS WITH CREAMY SPAM AND PASTA

INGREDIENTS:
- Sliced Real HORMENEL Bacon and 1 (12-ounce) can SPAM together to make a sandwich.

- 1 can (12 ounces) of SPAM Oven julienned roasted turkey breast
- 5 tablespoons of brown sugar that has been packed
- 30 to 40 wonton wrappers are required.
- 2 tablespoons Alfredo sauce (1-16-ounce container), split
- 2 cups elbow macaroni that has been cooked
- 1.1/2 cups shredded mozzarella cheese (about)
- 3/4 cup shredded Parmesan cheese, finely chopped
- 1/2 cup sun-dried tomatoes, finely chopped
- 1/4 cup chopped green onions.
- Vegetable oil is used for frying purposes.

INSTRUCTIONS:

1. Preheat the oven to 200 degrees Fahrenheit.
2. SPAM with Real HORMEL Bacon and SPAM Oven Roasted Turkey are combined in a big pan with a sprinkle of brown sugar, and the mixture is cooked until the bacon is crispy.
3. Cook the SPAM product over medium heat until it is golden brown, about 5 minutes.
4. Make triangles out of the wonton wrappers by cutting them diagonally in half.
5. Cook the wontons in heated oil until they are crisp and lightly browned, then drain on paper towels to remove excess fat.
6. Transfer the fried wontons to baking sheets and bake in the oven for 10 minutes.
7. Meanwhile, cook the Alfredo sauce in a skillet over medium heat. Once the sauce has been cooked, transfer it to a large mixing bowl and toss in 1 cup of warm Alfredo sauce and the macaroni.
8. The SPAM mixture, macaroni, cheese, and sun-dried tomatoes should be layered on top of the wontons.
9. Drizzle the leftover Alfredo sauce over the top.
10. Return the nachos to the oven and bake for another 5 minutes until the cheese is completely melted.
11. Onions should be placed on top of the nachos. Serve as soon as possible.

SPAMMY CAKES

INGREDIENTS:
- Chopped from 1 (12-ounce) can of SPAM Classic
- 1.1/2 cups all-purpose flour
- 1 teaspoon baking soda
- 1 cup granulated sugar
- a quarter teaspoon of salt
- 1.1/2 stick melted butter
- a half-gallon of milk
- 2 giant eggs (about)
- Divide the 2 teaspoons of vanilla extract in half.
- 3 medium potatoes, peeled and cooked in salted water
- 3 teaspoons of melted butter
- 3/4 cup confectioners' sugar

INSTRUCTIONS:
1. Preheat the oven to 350 degrees Fahrenheit.
2. Prepare a muffin pan by lining it with 12 cupcake liners.
3. Brown the SPAM Classic in a big pan until it is golden brown. Drain on a piece of paper towel.
4. Combine the flour, baking powder, sugar, and salt in a large mixing basin.
5. Stir in the SPAM Classic, reserving 1/4 cup for later until everything is well-combined.
6. Whisk together the melted butter, milk, eggs, and vanilla extract in a medium-sized mixing bowl. Add to the flour mixture and whisk until everything is well blended. Refrain from overworking the mixture.
7. Fill each cupcake liner halfway with batter—Bake for 20 to 25 minutes, or until the chicken is cooked. Remove from oven and allow rest in pan for 5 minutes before transferring to a wire rack to cool.

8. *Potatoes should be mashed until smooth. Stir in the butter with a fork until the butter is completely melted and the potatoes are soft. Add in the powdered sugar and mix well.*
9. *Fill a piping bag halfway with the mixture. The potato mixture should be piped onto the cakes. Sprinkle with the SPAM Classic that was set aside.*

RED ONION AND SLAW, SPAM STREET TACOS

INGREDIENTS:

- SPAM Classic, sliced into thin strips from two (12-ounce) cans
- 8 flour tortillas the size of street tacos
- 1/2 teaspoon freshly ground black pepper
- 1 garlic clove, peeled and minced
- 1/2 teaspoon freshly grated ginger, minced
- sauce (sweet chili sauce): 2 teaspoons
- 1/4 cup pickled red onion, prepared as directed
- green cabbage (2 cups) and red cabbage (2 cups) shredded 2 teaspoons minced jalapeno (2 tablespoons)
- 1/4 cup finely chopped cilantro
- a third of a cup of sour cream
- a third of a cup of buttermilk
- 1/2 cup apple cider vinegar.
- 3 teaspoons of table sugar
- 3 tablespoons lime juice
- a half teaspoon of cumin powder
- season with salt to taste

INSTRUCTIONS:

1. To make the cabbage slaw, combine the green cabbage, red cabbage, cilantro, and jalapeno in a large mixing bowl until well combined.
2. Whisk the remaining slaw ingredients in a separate mixing bowl until well combined.
3. Toss the slaw with the dressing until it is covered in the cabbage mixture. Refrigerate until ready to use as a topping for tacos.
4. Cook over medium-high heat, often stirring, until water thrown into the pan or griddle sizzles and evaporates.
5. In a large mixing bowl, combine the SPAM Classic strips and season with black pepper, garlic, ginger, and sweet chili sauce until the SPAM is well coated.
6. Sauté the seasoned SPAM Classic in a wok or on a griddle until the edges are crispy and the SPAM Classic is thoroughly cooked through. Remove from the oven and distribute among the street tacos.
7. Prepared cabbage slaw and a few pickled red onions should be placed on top of the sandwich. If desired, garnish with more cilantro to provide a finishing touch.

SPAM PHO

INGREDIENTS:
- a half (12-ounce) can of SPAM sliced teriyaki sauce
- 4 ounces uncooked rice noodles (not cooked)
- 3 cups chicken broth (preferably low in salt)
- the equivalent of 2 tablespoons of Hoisin Sauce from the HOUSE OF TSANG
- 2 tbsp. Freshly squeezed lime juice
- Fish sauce (about 1 tablespoon)
- 1/2 cup finely sliced white onion
- 1/2 cup fresh cilantro sprigs (about)
- 1/2 cup fresh Thai basil sprigs
- 1/4 cup sliced green onions

- *1 red chili pepper or red jalapeno, thinly sliced*

INSTRUCTIONS:

1. Cook the rice noodles according to the package instructions, then put them aside to cool.
2. Cook the SPAM Teriyaki slices according to the instructions on the box or until they are golden brown.
3. In a medium saucepan, simmer the chicken broth, HOUSE OF TSANG Hoisin Sauce, lime juice, and fish sauce over medium heat until the chicken is cooked through. Bring the mixture to a boil, remove it from the heat, and transfer it to the serving dishes.
4. Make a pile of noodles in each of the serving dishes. Finish with slices of SPAM Teriyaki and the other Ingredients.

CHEESECAKE WITH SPAM AND PINEAPPLE

INGREDIENTS:

FOR THE PURPOSE OF TRUST:

- 3 cups crushed oyster crackers
- 1 cup grated Parmesan cheese
- 1/3 cup melted butter

FOR THE FILLING:

- 3 cups smashed oyster crackers
- 1 cup grated Parmesan cheese
- chopped from 1 (12-ounce) can of SPAM Classic
- Softened cream cheese (four 8-ounce containers), four egg whites softly beaten
- Drain 1 can of pineapple tidbits in liquid (8 ounces) and set aside.

- 2 cups shredded Swiss cheese (or other similar cheese)
- 1/3 cup finely minced chives
- 1/4 cup finely diced fresh basil
- a quarter teaspoon of salt
- 1/4 teaspoon freshly ground white pepper
- a quarter teaspoon of garlic powder
- Crackers in various shapes and sizes

INSTRUCTIONS:

1. In a large mixing bowl, combine the oyster cracker crumbs, Parmesan cheese, and butter; leave aside 1/4 cup of the mixture for the topping.
2. Press the remaining crumb mixture into the bottom and up the sides of a greased 9-inch springform pan, about an inch up from the bottom. Refrigerate for at least 30 minutes after covering with plastic wrap.
3. Meanwhile, cook the SPAM Classic in a pan until it is gently browned, then remove it from the heat and put it aside.
4. A big mixing bowl should be used to combine all of the ingredients for this recipe. Add the eggs and mix on low speed until barely incorporated.
5. Mix in the SPAM Classic, pineapple, cheese, chives, basil, salt, pepper, and garlic powder until everything is well-combined. Mix until barely mixed, pour into the crust, and top with the remaining crumb mixture to make a beautiful presentation.
6. Place the pan on a baking sheet to catch any drips. Bake at 325°F for 70-90 minutes, or until the filling is nearly set, then remove from the oven and cool on a wire rack. Leave the cheesecake in the oven for 30 minutes, with the door slightly ajar to allow steam to escape.
7. Allow for 10 minutes of cooling time on a wire rack. To loosen the pan, carefully run a knife along the edge of the pan.
8. Allow for an extra hour of cooling time for the cheesecake. If you want to serve the cheesecake cooled, remove it from the pan and place it in the refrigerator overnight. Served warm or at room temperature, this dish is very delicious. Serve with a selection of crackers. This recipe serves 24-36 people.

CASSEROLE WITH POTATO PIEROGI WITH SPAM ADDED

INGREDIENTS:
- SPAM Classic (12-ounce can), chopped and sautéed in a skillet
- 2 tubs (each containing 24 ounces) of HORMEL mashed potatoes in an old-fashioned way
- cheese (about 2 cups shredded Cheddar)
- 1 cup sour cream
- 1 small onion, peeled and chopped (or split)
- a third of a cup melted butter, split
- Nine lasagna noodles have been cooked and cooled.

INSTRUCTIONS:
1. Preheat the oven to 350 degrees Fahrenheit.
2. Prepare a 9 x 13-inch baking pan with cooking spray.
3. Potatoes should be cooked according to the package instructions.
4. Pour the heated potatoes into a large mixing basin and stir in the cheese, sour cream, 3/4 of the SPAM Classic, and the onion until everything is thoroughly combined.
5. Two tablespoons of butter should be spread onto the bottom of the baking pan.
6. Place 3 lasagna sheets in a single layer on the melted butter and set aside.
7. Place a third of the potato mixture on top of each lasagna sheet.
8. Repeat the layers of lasagna and potatoes a second time.
9. Pour the remaining butter over the potatoes and toss to combine.
10. Add the leftover SPAM Classic to finish it off.
11. 30-40 minutes, or until the potatoes are heated and bubbling, bake covered with aluminum foil.

12. Remove the pan from the oven and set it aside for 10 minutes before slicing the cake.

BURGER WITH SPAM AND RAMEN

INGREDIENTS:
- 1 packet (3 ounces) of ramen noodle soup
- 1 large egg that has been gently beaten
- canola oil (around 1 tablespoon)
- 1 package (3 ounces) of SPAM Single
- 2 tablespoons kimchi that has been drained

INSTRUCTIONS:
1. Prepare the noodles according to the package instructions, including the spice packet. The liquid should be drained and discarded. Allow noodles to sit for 15 minutes.
2. After mixing in the egg, split the mixture in half.
3. Bowls should be lined with two pieces of plastic wrap and a layer of noodles. Wrap the noodles in plastic wrap and weigh them down with similar-sized dishes. Refrigerate for 2 hours, then take the noodles from the plastic wrapper.
4. Heat the oil in a large skillet over medium heat. Cook ramen patties in oil for 2 to 3 minutes on each side, depending on their thickness. Carefully transfer to a serving platter.
5. Cook the SPAM slice for 2 to 3 minutes until it begins to color. One ramen patty should be topped with a spam slice and kimchi. Add the remaining ramen patty on top.

BISCUITS WITH SPAM, BACON, EGGS, AND CHEESE

INGREDIENTS:
- 1 (12-ounce) can SPAM with REAL HORMEL Bacon, sliced into eight slices
- Eight slices each of American, Swiss, or sharp cheese. Cheddar cheese is a kind of cheese.
- 4 big quail eggs
- 1 can of biscuit dough that has been chilled

INSTRUCTIONS:
1. Bake the biscuits according to the instructions on the box.
2. Meanwhile, cook the SPAM with Real HORMEL Bacon in a pan until it is crispy, then remove the SPAM with Real HORMEL Bacon from the skillet.
3. Scramble the eggs in the same pan as the bacon.
4. Divide the biscuits in half and stack the bottom halves with eggs, cheese, SPAM with Real HORMEL Bacon, and then the top halves of the biscuits on top of the bottom.

SANDWICH MADE WITH GRILLED CHEESE AND EGGS AND SPAM

INGREDIENTS:
- 2 slices of SPAM, single-serving size
- 2 pieces of sourdough bread
- 1 piece of cheddar cheese
- 1 big egg (about)

INSTRUCTIONS:
1. Fry the SPAM Singles in a small pan over medium-high heat for approximately 15 minutes, flipping once halfway through the cooking time.
2. Cook the egg in a small pan until it reaches the desired doneness.
3. Butter one side of each piece of bread and set it aside.

4. Please place them in a pan butter-side down and cover with cheese, one piece at a time.
5. Cook until the cheese has begun to melt and the bread has begun to toast.
6. SPAM and an egg are placed on top of the cheese. Top with the top piece of bread.

MUSUBI BITES WITH ADOBO FRIED RICE AND SPAM

INGREDIENTS:
- One can (12 ounces) of SPAM Sodium is reduced by chopping it up tiny.
- 1/4 cup finely diced onion
- 2 garlic cloves, peeled and chopped
- a quarter cup of apple cider vinegar
- 1/4 cup white vinegar
- 2 teaspoons of distilled water
- 1 bay leaf
- a half teaspoon of freshly cracked black pepper
- 2 tbsp soy sauce
- Oyster sauce (about 2 tablespoons)
- 2 tablespoons brown sugar
- green onion (about 1/4 cup) sliced
- 2 scrambled eggs
- 3 cups sushi rice that has been cooked
- 4 nori sheets, each half-sheeted

INSTRUCTIONS:
1. Cook SPAM Less Sodium for 2 to 3 minutes, or until golden brown, in a large pan over medium-high heat until golden brown. Cook for 1 to 2 minutes, or until the onions are soft until the garlic is fragrant. Combine the apple cider, white vinegar,

water, bay leaf, and black pepper in a large saucepan. Turn down the heat. Stirring constantly, cook for 1 to 2 minutes, or until the liquid decreases. Combine the soy, oyster, and brown sugar in a mixing bowl. Cook for 1 to 2 minutes, or until the sauce has thickened somewhat, stirring constantly.
2. Combine the green onions, eggs, and cooked rice in a large mixing bowl—Stir-fry for 1 to 2 minutes, or until everything is thoroughly blended and hot. Remove the pan from the heat. Remove the bay leaf from the dish.
3. Place 1/2 cup of the rice mixture into a musubi press or a SPAM Less Sodium can lined with plastic wrap and press down. Remove from the press and place on top of a nori sheet that has been halved. Wrap the Nori around the musubi, moistening the edge of the Nori to help it stick together. Make another eight by repeating the process. Each should be cut into bite-sized pieces.

SPAMLT

INGREDIENTS:
- 1 (12-ounce) can SPAM Classic, split into 8 equal portions
- 8 pieces of sourdough bread, lightly buttered
- 8 butter lettuce leaves, well cleaned
- 1/2 cup mayonnaise
- Tomatoes cut into 8 pieces
- canola oil (around 1 tablespoon)

INSTRUCTIONS:
1. Cook the SPAM Classic slices in a large pan over medium heat until they are golden brown on both sides.
2. Spread mayonnaise on one side of each bread slice and toast until golden brown.
3. Over four pieces of bread, arrange the remaining lettuce leaves, tomato slices, and two SPAM Classic slices as desired.

4. Spread mayonnaise on one side of the bread and top with the other.

SANDWICH WITH SPAM (KATSU)

INGREDIENTS:
- a half cup of flour
- 2 eggs, lightly beaten
- 1 cup bread crumbs made from panko bread crumbs and 2 teaspoons white sesame seeds
- 1 can (12 ounces) of SPAM Traditionally prepared, cut into four pieces. Vegetable oil
- 4 tablespoons hot mustard
- 8 slices of thick white bread gently toasted on both sides
- okonomiyaki sauce (about 2 tablespoons)
- 12 dill pickles cut into thin slices
- 4 oz. shredded American cheese

INSTRUCTIONS:
1. Prepare three shallow plates by separating the flour, eggs, and breadcrumbs. Breadcrumbs may be used to coat SPAM Classic slices after being dredged in flour.
2. One inch of vegetable oil should be poured into a big pan to cover the bottom. Heat the oil over medium-high heat until shimmering. Cook the breaded SPAM Classic slices in a pan for 2 to 3 minutes, flipping once or until golden brown, depending on their thickness. Remove the skillet from the heat.
3. Four pieces of bread should be slathered with spicy mustard. Using the remaining bread pieces, spread the okonomiyaki sauce over them. Place pickles on top of hot mustard and cheese on top of okonomiyaki; sandwich with breaded SPAM Classic to make an okonomiyaki sandwich. Cut the crusts in half after trimming them.

SPAM SALAD WITH A BOW TIE

INGREDIENTS:
- SPAM Classic, sliced into julienne pieces, 1 (12-ounce) can
- blanched broccoli florets (about 2 cups)
- 2 cups bow tie pasta, fully cooked
- 1/4 cup finely diced bell pepper
- 1/4 cup finely chopped onion
- 1/4 cup vegetable oil
- 1/4 cup white wine vinegar
- 3 tablespoons Dijon mustard with honey
- grated Parmesan cheese (about 2 tablespoons)
- 1 garlic clove, peeled and minced

INSTRUCTIONS:
1. Brown the SPAM Classic in a big pan until it is lightly browned on both sides.
2. Combine the SPAM Classic, broccoli, spaghetti, bell pepper, and onion in a large non-metal mixing bowl until thoroughly combined.
3. In a separate bowl, combine the other ingredients with a wire whisk or fork until well combined, then add to the SPAM mixture and thoroughly blend.
4. Refrigerate for several hours or overnight after covering with plastic wrap.

CHOWDER WITH SPAM AND POTATOES

INGREDIENTS:

- chopped from 1 (12-ounce) can of SPAM Classic
- butter or margarine (around 1 tablespoon)
- Caraway seeds (about 1/2 teaspoon)
- 1/2 cup celery, finely chopped
- 1/4 cup fresh parsley, finely chopped
- 1.1/2 cups half-and-half (10.7-ounce can) condensed chicken broth
- 1 medium onion, peeled and sliced
- 1/4 teaspoon freshly ground pepper
- potato cubes (about 3 medium potatoes) 1-pound (approximately 3 medium potatoes), peeled and diced
- 1 cup of distilled water

INSTRUCTIONS:
1. In a medium-sized saucepan, sauté the onion and celery in the butter until they are soft.
2. Cook for 3 minutes, stirring regularly, until the SPAM Classic is heated.
3. Combine the broth, water, potatoes, caraway seeds, and pepper in a saucepan.
4. Cook for 10 minutes, or until potatoes are cooked, covered with a lid.
5. Add the half-and-half and parsley and heat until ready to serve.

SLOPPY JOES WITH SPAMBURGER

INGREDIENTS:
- 1 can of SPAM Lite (12 ounces)
- 1 cup barbecue sauce
- 6 hamburger buns that have been divided and toasted
- 6 slices (about 3/4-pound) of mozzarella cheese
- 1 medium onion, peeled and sliced

INSTRUCTIONS:

1. Cook the SPAM Lite in a medium saucepan over medium-low heat, stirring for 5 to 7 minutes, or until the SPAM Lite is heated. Stir the mixture constantly.
2. Fill the buns with the SPAM mixture.
3. Sprinkle the cheese and onion on top in an equal layer.

TURKEY ROLLUPS WITH SPAM

INGREDIENTS:

- 1 can (12 ounces) of SPAM Turkey breast that has been oven roasted and thinly sliced
- 6 (10-inch) CHI-CHI'S flour tortillas are large enough to serve as burritos.
- 3/4 cup garden veggie cream cheese (without the fat).
- lettuce with 6 leaves
- 4 Roma tomatoes, cut very thinly

INSTRUCTIONS:

1. Two tablespoons of cream cheese should be spread over each tortilla.
2. SPAM Oven Roasted Turkey, lettuce, and tomato are placed on top.
3. Make a roll and place it in the refrigerator until you are ready to serve.
4. To serve, cut rollups in half diagonally or set wooden picks 1 inch apart for appetizers and slice them into slices.

SLT FOR THE ULTIMATE SPAM BREAKFAST

INGREDIENTS:
- One 12-ounce can of SPAM Classic, cut into eight slices,
- cut 4 Roma tomatoes lengthwise in half, and set them aside.
- 1 tablespoon extra-virgin olive oil
- a half teaspoon of garlic powder, divided half a teaspoon of salt, divided half a teaspoon of pepper, and split two tablespoons of sugar
- 1 tablespoon fresh basil leaves, finely chopped
- 3/4 cup mayonnaise (about)
- pitted 1 avocado, peeled, and mashed
- 8 English muffins, slashed and lightly toasted
- Spinach greens that have been freshly harvested
- 8 eggs, poached sunny-side up, in a skillet

INSTRUCTIONS:
1. Preheat the oven to 450 degrees Fahrenheit.
2. Prepare a baking sheet with a rim by lining it with parchment paper. Place SPAM slices on one half of the baking sheet and set aside.
3. Arrange the Roma tomatoes cut side up on the opposite half of the baking sheet. Sprinkle the tomatoes with olive oil, 1/2 teaspoon garlic powder, 1/2 teaspoon salt, 1/4 teaspoon pepper, sugar, and basil, and toss to combine.
4. Baking time will be 25 to 30 minutes, or until the SPAM Classic is crisped and browned and the tomatoes are softened, with the dish rotating once throughout cooking.
5. In a small mixing bowl, combine the mayonnaise, avocado, the remaining 1/4 teaspoon garlic powder, the remaining 1/4 teaspoon salt, and the remaining 1/4 teaspoon pepper until everything is thoroughly blended.
6. Spread the avocado mixture over the English muffins that have been cut in half. Fill the bottom half of the muffin pan with spinach leaves, 1 SPAM piece, 1 tomato, 1 egg, and the top of the muffin pan.

SPAM HOT CHEESY PARTY DIP

INGREDIENTS:
- 1 (12-ounce) can SPAM Classic, sliced into thin strips
- 2 (8-ounce) packages of cream cheese that have been softened
- a third cup of milk
- onion coarsely chopped (about 1/4 cup)
- 2 tablespoons horseradish that has been prepared
- 8 drops of spicy pepper sauce

INSTRUCTIONS:
1. Preheat the oven to 375 degrees Fahrenheit.
2. Cook SPAM Classic in a large pan over medium-high heat until gently browned, about 5 minutes.
3. Meanwhile, in a large mixing bowl, combine the cream cheese and milk until smooth.
4. Combine the onion, horseradish, spicy sauce, and half of the SPAM Classic in a mixing bowl.
5. Fill an 11-by-7-inch baking dish with the SPAM mixture. Half of the SPAM Classic should be sprinkled on the cream cheese mixture.
6. Bake for 20 to 25 minutes until the mixture is hot and bubbling.
7. If desired, garnish with thinly sliced green onions. Serve with French bread to mop up the sauce.

TACOS WITH SPAM

INGREDIENTS:
- 1 (12-ounce) can SPAM Jalapeno pepper, finely chopped
- 1/2 cup washed and drained canned black beans
- taco shells made with yellow corn, cooked with 1/2 cup canned corn that has been drained

- Shredded lettuce
- Tomatoes, finely diced
- Queso Fresco is a cheese from Mexico.
- Salsa, sour cream, and a WHOLE guacamole dip

INSTRUCTIONS:

1. Sauté the SPAM Jalapenos in a large pan until they are lightly browned.
2. Cook until the black beans and corn are warmed, about 5 minutes.
3. Fill taco shells with the SPAM mixture while they are still heated.
4. Tacos should be topped with shredded lettuce, chopped tomatoes, and cheese.
5. If desired, serve with salsa, sour cream, and guacamole to complete the meal.

HAWAII KABOBS WITH SPAM CORDON BLEU

INGREDIENTS:

- 1 can (12 ounces) of SPAM less sodium, cut into 1-1/2-inch chunks less sodium
- 2 quarts of water
- 1/4 cup pineapple juice
- 1.1/2 cups cooked rice
- 3/3 cup roughly chopped macadamia nuts, to taste
- chopped parsley (about a third of a cup)
- 1 cup pineapple preserves
- vinegar from white wine (about 2 teaspoons).
- 1 teaspoon red pepper flakes (crushed)
- To taste, season with salt and freshly ground pepper.
- 1-1/2-inch-thick slices of pineapple, peeled and cored
- 1-1/2-inch slices of red onion, peeled and chopped

- 6 bamboo skewers, soaked in water for 30 minutes, twisted together
- Using olive oil to wash your teeth
- 1 cup shredded Swiss cheese, preferably fresh

INSTRUCTIONS:

1. In a medium saucepan, mix the water and the juice and bring to a boil. Bring the water to a boil.
2. Stir in the rice until it is evenly distributed. Reduce the heat to a low setting. Cook for 20 minutes with the lid on, then fluff with a fork.
3. Stir in the nuts and parsley until everything is well-combined. Remove from the oven and keep warm.
4. Cook over medium heat for 3 minutes, or until the preserves, vinegar, and red pepper with salt and pepper are heated, stirring periodically, to form the pineapple glaze in a small saucepan with the salt and pepper.
5. Preheat the grill to medium heat.
6. SPAM in the thread Using less sodium, pineapple, and onion are skewered together. Using a pastry brush, coat the surface with oil and season with salt and pepper.
7. 10 to 12 minutes, they were flipped regularly until hot and grill marks developed. Brush with pineapple glaze halfway through cooking time. Swiss cheese should be sprinkled over hot kebabs. Serve with macadamia rice to complete the meal.

BREAKFAST HASH WITH SPAM

INGREDIENTS:

- chopped from 1 (12-ounce) can of SPAM Classic
- 2 tbsp. extra-virgin olive oil
- 1/4 cup finely chopped fresh parsley
- 1/4 teaspoon freshly ground pepper
- 1 medium onion, finely chopped
- 2 big baked potatoes, peeled and diced

- *12 red bell pepper, diced*
- *12 green bell pepper, diced*
- *1/4 teaspoon freshly ground pepper*

INSTRUCTIONS:
1. *Heat the oil in a 10-inch cast-iron pan over medium heat until shimmering.*
2. *Cook for 3 minutes, or until the onions are transparent.*
3. *Cook for 7 to 10 minutes until the potatoes are golden brown.*
4. *Cook, stirring, until the SPAM Classic, red and green peppers, and bell peppers are cooked and browned.*
5. *Add the chopped parsley and pepper and mix well.*

THAI SALAD CUPS WITH SPAM

INGREDIENTS:
- *12-ounce can SPAM Classic (cut into cubes), drained and rinsed*
- *2 teaspoons freshly peeled and minced ginger root*
- *3 garlic cloves, peeled and minced*
- *1 tablespoon extra-virgin olive oil*
- *1/4 cup coarsely chopped fresh mint*
- *1 tablespoon freshly squeezed lime juice*
- *1 tablespoon toasted sesame seeds*
- *a half teaspoon of red pepper flakes (crushed)*
- *4 cups mixed salad greens*

INSTRUCTIONS:
1. *Cook the ginger root and garlic in oil for 2 minutes in a pan over medium heat.*
2. *Sauté for another 4 minutes after adding SPAM Classic.*

3. Mix the mint, lime juice, sesame seeds, and red pepper flakes in a pan and cook for 30 seconds.
4. Distribute the dressing over the salad leaves.

TURKEY POT PIE WITH SPAM

INGREDIENTS:
- Oven Roasted Turkey, chopped into tiny bits,
- 1 (12-ounce) can SPAM, cut into small portions
- 16-ounce package of phyllo dough (thawed), if desired
- 1-pound frozen mixed veggies
- 1 (10-ounce) can of cream of chicken soup (with reduced-fat milk)
- 1/4 teaspoon freshly ground white pepper
- 1/2 cup skim milk

INSTRUCTIONS:
1. Preheat the oven to 375 degrees Fahrenheit.
2. Prepare a large deep-dish pie plate by arranging 6 to 8 layers of phyllo dough in a circular pattern in the pan and spraying each layer with cooking spray before baking.
3. Combine the SPAM Oven and the other ingredients in a large mixing dish. Roasted Turkey, mixed veggies, Soup, milk, and white pepper are all served with this dish. Pour over the phyllo sheets that have been stacked.
4. Place 10 more phyllo layers in a circular pattern on top of the SPAM mixture, spraying each layer with cooking spray between each layer.
5. Fold the sides of the phyllo up and over the edge of the pie pan; crimp the edges together.
6. Thirty minutes until the filling is bubbly and the crust is crisp and golden, or 25 to 30 minutes longer. If the edge of the pastry begins to brown, cover it with aluminum foil.

MUSUBIS WITH SPICED CHILLI AND GARLIC

INGREDIENTS:
- One can of SPAM (12 ounces) Make 8 slices of Hot & Spicy, cut lengthwise.
- Cooked white steamed rice (4.5 ounces) in advance of serving
- cut four sheets of Japanese Nori into halves
- Olive oil (1 ounce) is a kind of oil that is produced by pressing olives.
- garlic, minced (2 tablespoons)
- Chili paste and Sambal oelek (about 2 teaspoons each)
- Mirin, 1/4 cup –
- Water in one ounce
- Honey (around 12 tablespoons)
- to taste freshly ground black pepper

INSTRUCTIONS:
1. Light oil should be heated in a medium-sized sauté pan.
2. Cook the SPAM Hot & Spicy on all sides for 2-3 minutes, then remove from the pan and set aside.
3. Garlic and chili paste should be cooked together in the same pan for around 1 minute or until the garlic is fully cooked.
4. Cook for 3-4 minutes, adding water, mirin, and honey as needed.
5. Cook the SPAM Hot & Spicy in the pan until the sauce clings to the SPAM mixture (about 5 minutes).
6. After you've finished cooking, season with black pepper, then arrange on a bed of rice and cover with Nori. Warm up the dish before serving it to guests.

SPAM LOCO MOCO

INGREDIENTS:

- 2 slices each of 1 (12-ounce) can of SPAM Classic
- 2 teaspoons of melted butter
- 1 cup cremini mushrooms, finely chopped
- 1 cup finely diced sweet onion
- Beef broth (two cups) and two tablespoons of Worcestershire sauce
- 2 tablespoons cornstarch
- 3 teaspoons of distilled water
- 4 cups of rice that has been cooked
- 2 hard-boiled eggs, done sunny side up
- 3 tablespoons of finely chopped parsley from Italy
- If preferred, add 1/4 cup diced Roma tomato to the mix. 3 teaspoons chopped green onion

INSTRUCTIONS:

1. Cook the SPAM Classic in a large pan over medium heat for 3 to 5 minutes, or until it is gently browned and crunchy. Remove the skillet from the heat.
2. Melt the butter in the same skillet. Cook the mushrooms and onions for 6 to 8 minutes, or until they are golden brown and soft, over medium-high heat, stirring often.
3. Add the beef stock and Worcestershire sauce to boil the mushroom mixture.
4. Combine cornstarch and water in a small bowl until a homogeneous paste is formed. Add to the pan and whisk until everything is well mixed and thickened.
5. Season with salt and pepper to your liking.
6. Rice should be divided among four plates. Place 2 slices of SPAM Classic on top of the rice. Gravy and 1 egg should be placed on top.
7. If preferred, garnish with parsley, green onion, and tomato, or serve as is

MINI SPAM NACHO BURGERS

INGREDIENTS:
- 3 Roma tomatoes, peeled and diced
- 3-tablespoons red onion, finely diced
- 3 tablespoons of red wine vinegar
- 2 tablespoons finely chopped Peppers in Adobo Sauce with EMBASE Chipotle Peppers
- 2 tablespoons of honey
- 1 can (12 ounces) of SPAM Classic, sliced into six pieces
- 6 tiny buns, divided and gently toasted
- 3 slices of cheddar cheese, sliced in half
- 3 small rolls, split and lightly toasted
- 1 cup WHOLLY Classic Guacamole (serves 4-6 people)
- a total of six slices of Green Jalapeno Wheels from CHI-CHI'S

INSTRUCTIONS:
1. To create the salsa, combine the tomatoes, onion, vinegar, and chipotle in adobo sauce and honey in a large mixing basin.
2. Grill or grill SPAM Classic until it is nicely cooked on both sides, about 2 minutes each. Add cheese to the top of the SPAM Classic and cook until the cheese starts to melt.
3. One slice of SPAM Classic should be placed on the bottom half of each roll. Add guacamole, salsa, and a jalapeno slice to each burger. Roll up the tops of the rolls to protect them.

SPAM FRIED TO DELICIOUSNESS!

INGREDIENTS:
- One can (12 ounces) of SPAM. To make teriyaki, dice
- 2 tablespoons vegetable oil, divided
- Two eggs, and whisk together.
- 1/4 cup grated carrots, diced
- a quarter cup of finely chopped green onions
- 1/4 cup thawed frozen peas
- 1/4 cup red bell pepper, finely chopped

- *2 cups of rice, cooked*
- *a total of three tablespoons of SOY SAUCE FROM THE HOUSE OF TSANG*

INSTRUCTIONS:
1. One tablespoon of oil should be heated in a big pan.
2. In a separate bowl, whisk together the eggs. Cook, constantly stirring, until the desired doneness is reached. Remove the skillet from the heat and put it aside.
3. Heat the remaining 1 tablespoon of oil in the same skillet. SPAM should be prepared in advance. Cook for 4 minutes, or until veggies are soft, with the Teriyaki, carrots, green onions, and bell pepper.
4. Combine the rice and egg in a large mixing bowl. Soy sauce should be sprinkled on top. Make sure to heat everything thoroughly.
5. Season with salt and pepper, and garnish with extra green onion.

MUSUBI WITH TERIYAKI KATSU AND SPAM

INGREDIENTS:
- 8-10 slices of 1 (12-ounce) can get SPAM Teriyaki sliced lengthwise from the can
- 4.5 ounces of white steamed rice that has been prepared ahead of time
- cut in half 5 sheets of Japanese Nori (

Nori)

- 1-ounce extra-virgin olive oil
- 6 cups Japanese Panko (also known as bread crumbs)
- 4 quail eggs
- Mochiko flour (Japanese rice flour) 1 cup

INSTRUCTIONS:
1. Heat the oil in a medium-sized sauté pan over medium heat, then sear the SPAM Teriyaki on both sides for 2-3 minutes.
2. Place on a bed of rice and cover with Nori.
3. After that, use the standard breading procedure: flour, egg, and finally, Panko. Heat the oil to 350°F for 2-3 minutes, or until the batter is golden brown.
4. Serve immediately to ensure crispness.

SPAMBURGER HAMBURGER

INGREDIENTS:
- 1 (12-ounce) can SPAM Classic (or similar)
- 4 hamburger buns, cut in half
- 4 lettuce leaves (about)
- If desired, 4 pieces of cheese may be used.
- Ketchup

INSTRUCTIONS:
1. Preparation of the grill
2. SPAM Classic should be cut into four pieces.
3. Preheat the grill to medium heat and flip it once every 5 to 7 minutes, or until the SPAM Classic is well cooked.
4. Before taking the SPAM Classic from the grill, place a piece of cheese on each slice of SPAM Classic.

SPAM SPUDS

INGREDIENTS:

- 6 big baking potatoes (about)
- 1 package frozen broccoli and carrots in herb sauce, thawed and chopped into smaller pieces
- 1 package of frozen broccoli and carrots in herb sauce
- 1 can (12 ounces) of SPAM Oven Diced roasted turkey breast
- 1 can fiesta nacho cheese soup (about)
- 1 can of cheddar cheese soup (from a can)
- with peppers, 1 cup shredded Monterey Jack cheese
- 1 cup chopped bacon
- season with salt and pepper to taste
- green onions, sliced or diced to taste

INSTRUCTIONS:

1. Preheat the oven to 375 degrees Fahrenheit.
2. Wrap the potatoes in aluminum foil after piercing them with a fork—Bake for 1 hour, or until the potatoes are tender.
3. Prepare the veggies according to the instructions on the box. SPAM Oven should be included. Soups and roasted turkey are on the menu.
4. Potatoes should be cut the long way—season with salt and pepper after stirring the meat's interior. Spoon in a little amount of the SPAM mixture and toss.
5. More SPAM mixture should be added. Cheese and onions should be sprinkled on top.

BISCUITS WITH JALAPENOS

INGREDIENTS:

- half a pound SPAM with real HORMEL Bacon, diced
- all-purpose flour (about 5 ounces)
- baking powder (about a third of an ounce)
- 5 ounces of all-purpose flour

- sugar (half an ounce)
- 1 pinch of table salt
- 6 a half-ounce of milk
- 3 1/2 ounces of shortening (or butter) or margarine
- a half cup of shredded sharp cheddar cheese is a kind of cheese.
- peppers, seeded and diced: 1 jalapeno pepper
- 1 medium-sized egg, softly whisked with a few drops of water

INSTRUCTIONS:

1. "Preheat the oven to 425 degrees Fahrenheit.
2. Prepare a baking sheet by lining it with parchment paper or spraying it with cooking spray.
3. Cook SPAM with Real HORMEL Bacon in a pan over medium-high heat until gently browned, about 5 minutes.
4. Dry Ingredients should be sifted together in a large mixing basin. Using a pastry blender, blend in the butter until the mixture resembles coarse cornmeal.
5. Pour in the milk. Continue to mix until a soft dough is produced.
6. Combine the SPAM product, cheese, and jalapenos in a small mixing bowl until barely mixed. MAKE SURE NOT TO OVERMIX!
7. Lightly knead the dough 10 times, or for approximately 20 seconds, until it is soft and somewhat elastic but does not get sticky.
8. Roll out the dough to a thickness of 1 inch, ensuring it is consistent throughout.
9. Cut out biscuits to minimize waste by pushing the cutter straight down without rotating the blade (twisting will interfere with rising).
10. Place biscuits on a baking sheet 1/2 inch apart and brush with egg wash to finish.
11. Bake biscuits for about 15 minutes, flipping the baking sheet halfway through. "

MUSUBI WITH SPAM

INGREDIENTS:

- 3 ounces cooked white rice, seasoned with furikake and toasted sesame seeds if desired
- 2 slices SPAM Classic – cut 3,
- 8 ounces cooked white rice, seasoned with furikake and toasted sesame seeds if desired
- The amount equal to one tablespoon of HOUSE OF TSANG Hibachi Grill Sweet Ginger Sesame Sauce or HOUSE OF TSANG General Tso Sauce is two famous sauces for Hibachi Grill.
- 1 nori sheet in its entirety

INSTRUCTIONS:

1. Cook SPAM Classic in a big pan until it is gently toasted and crisp, about 5 minutes. Grill sauce or cooking sauce should be drizzled on top.
2. Alternatively, line the interior of an empty SPAM Classic can work with plastic wrap and set the rice into the can to make a musubi press. Firmly press the rice into the bottom of the pan.
3. Top with seasoned furikake and toasted sesame seeds, or serve plain.
4. Place SPAM Classic on rice in a press or a can and push down. Firmly press your fingers into the ground. Optional: sprinkle the leftover rice on top and press down.
5. Take the SPAM Classic and rice out of the musubi press or container and set them aside.
6. Nori should be cut to the required width on a work surface.
7. Cover with pressed SPAM Classic and rice and arrange the nori shiny-side-down. Wrap Nori around a pressed SPAM Classic and a small handful of rice. Serve as soon as possible.

FRITTATA WITH SPAM

INGREDIENTS:

- 1 can (seven-ounce) SPAM Classic, diced
- 3 tablespoons of vegetable oil, split

- 2 big potatoes, cooked, skinned, and cubed
- 10 pitted ripe olives, chopped
- 6 large eggs
- 1/2 cup onion, finely chopped
- 1/2 cup green bell pepper, coarsely chopped
- 2 teaspoons of distilled water
- a quarter teaspoon of salt
- 1/4 teaspoon freshly ground pepper

INSTRUCTIONS:

1. The onion and bell pepper should be sautéed until gently browned in an omelet pan or skillet with a 10-inch diameter and 2 teaspoons of oil.
2. Cook over low heat, stirring regularly, for 5 minutes until the SPAM Classic, potatoes, and olives are heated.
3. Remove the food from the pan's bottom by squeezing it.
4. Tilt the pan to coat the bottom with 1 tablespoon of oil and set aside.
5. Whisk together the eggs, water, salt, and black pepper in a large mixing bowl. Pour the mixture over the SPAM mixture.
6. Cover the pan and simmer for 15 minutes or until the frittata is set on the bottom. Using a pancake turner, release the edge and base of the pancake and flip it onto a serving tray to finish.

PAELLA WITH SPAM

INGREDIENTS:

- 1 can (12 ounces) of SPAM
- 1/4 cup extra virgin olive oil, diced for less sodium
- 1 garlic clove, minced
- 1 white onion, chopped
- 1 red bell pepper, diced
- 1 green bell pepper, diced
- 1 to 2 pinches of saffron strands
- 3 tablespoons tomato paste.

- cooked rice
- 3 teaspoons chopped pimento
- 3 cups cooked quinoa

INSTRUCTIONS:
1. Cook the Spam Less Sodium in a large pan over medium-high heat for 3 to 4 minutes, or until it is gently browned. Cook, constantly stirring, for 2 to 3 minutes, or until the onions are softened, until the oil is hot.
2. Cook for 2 minutes after adding the bell peppers and saffron. Stir in the tomato paste until everything is well-combined. Add in the rice and mix well. Pimiento is used as a garnish.

SPAM BARS

INGREDIENTS:
- 1 (12-ounce) can SPAM Classic (or similar)
- 1/4 cup granulated sugar
- 1/4 cup maple syrup
- split into two halves, 1/1/2 teaspoon of ground cinnamon
- 1/4 cup candied pecans, finely sliced
- a half teaspoon of sea salt
- One cup of dark chocolate melting chocolates (dark chocolate is preferred).

INSTRUCTIONS:
1. Preheat the oven to 400 degrees Fahrenheit.
2. Piece the SPAM Classic into 16 bar-shaped slices and arrange each portion on a baking sheet lined with parchment paper.
3. In a small mixing bowl, combine the brown sugar, maple syrup, and 1 teaspoon of cinnamon until well combined.
4. Spread the mixture over all 16 slices of SPAM Classic in a uniform layer.
5. Bake for 15 minutes, then remove from the oven and flip the slices over to cook on the other side.

6. Brush the slices with extra glaze and bake for 15 minutes before transferring them to a cooling rack lined with parchment paper.
7. While the SPAM Classic slices are cooling, prepare the topping by combining the chopped nuts, sea salt, and 1/2 teaspoon cinnamon in a small dish and set aside until needed.
8. Melt both chocolates in a double boiler, constantly stirring, until smooth.
9. Each piece of candied SPAM Classic should be dipped in the molten chocolate until completely covered on both sides, using tongs.
10. Spread the pecan mixture on a baking sheet with wax paper and bake for 30 minutes.
11. Refrigerate for 10 minutes before serving or until the cheese has set. This recipe yields 16 bars. Refrigerate after opening.

SPAMBURGERTM WITH HAWAIIAN SPAMBURGERTM SAUCE

INGREDIENTS:
- 1 (12-ounce) can SPAM Classic (or similar)
- 1-eight-ounce-can pineapple slices in their juice
- If desired, 4 sliced green bell pepper may be substituted.
- 1/4 cup creamy mustard mix (or equivalent)
- 1 garlic clove, peeled and cut
- 4 hamburger buns that have been divided and toasted
- Lettuce (four leaves)
- If desired, 4 slices of Swiss cheese may be substituted.

INSTRUCTIONS:
1. Preparation of the grill
2. SPAM Classic should be cut into four pieces.
3. Grill the SPAM Classic, pineapple, and bell pepper on a grill pan, stirring once, for 5 to 7 minutes, or until the SPAM Classic is heated.

4. In a mixing dish, combine the mustard mixture and garlic; distribute over the cut sides of the buns to serve. Fill each bun with lettuce, SPAM Classic, pineapple, bell pepper, and cheese, alternating between the two buns.

HOT BROWNS WITH SPAM

INGREDIENTS:
- 1 (12-ounce) can SPAM Classic, sliced into 6 equal portions
- butter (about 1.1/2 tbsp)
- 15 tablespoons of unbleached all-purpose flour
- spicy pepper sauce (about 1/2 tsp)
- 1.1/2 cups whole milk or heavy cream, whichever you choose
- 1/2 teaspoon Worcestershire sauce is a condiment.
- 1 cup shredded white cheddar cheese, preferably aged
- 6 pieces of solid white bread or oatmeal bread, toasted to your liking
- 6 big tomato slices, sliced thinly
- 12 slices of HORMEL BLACK LABEL that has been fried HORMEL or BAKED BACON Bacon that has been thoroughly cooked
- season with freshly ground black pepper to taste
- garnished with finely chopped fresh parsley

INSTRUCTIONS:
1. Melt the butter in a large saucepan over medium heat to make the sauce.
2. Cook, constantly stirring, over medium heat for approximately 2 minutes, until the flour is lightly browned and bubbling, whichever comes first.
3. Over medium heat, heat and constantly whisk until the sauce has thickened, adding more milk or cream if necessary to achieve desired consistency.
4. Remove the pan from the heat and toss the cheese until it is completely melted. Keep the dish warm and put it aside.
5. Preheat the oven to 350 degrees Fahrenheit for the Hot Browns.

6. Heat the SPAM Classic in a large pan over medium heat until nicely browned on both sides.
7. Arrange the toasted bread pieces in a baking dish that has been oven-proofed.
8. SPAM Classic and tomato slices are placed on top.
9. Season the tomatoes with freshly ground black pepper.
10. Place a spoonful of the prepared cheese sauce on top of each.
11. Place in the oven for about 5 minutes, or until the top is gently browned.
12. To finish, top with two slices of bacon and fresh chopped parsley on each plate. This recipe serves 6.

APPLE'S SPAM TURNOVER

INGREDIENTS:
- a half-cup of diced SPAM Classic
- 2 tablespoons cornstarch
- 1-pound cream cheese, whipped
- 1 cup apple, peeled and diced
- 1/2 cup cranberries, defrosted
- 1 box of thawed puff pastry sheets from a freezer package
- 3/4 cup granulated sugar
- 1/2 cup brown sugar that has been packed
- 1 teaspoon pure vanilla extract
- a half cup of water

INSTRUCTIONS:
1. Preheat the oven to 350 degrees Fahrenheit.
2. In a medium-sized saucepan, combine the apple, granulated sugar, brown sugar, cranberries, and water until well combined.
3. Bring to a low boil over medium heat, stirring constantly.
4. Remove the pan from the heat and stir in the SPAM Classic, cornstarch, and vanilla until well combined.

5. Cook over medium heat until the sauce has thickened, then remove from the heat and set aside to cool for a few minutes.
6. Puff pastry should be cut into pieces of 3 34 inches in length.
7. In the middle of each square, place a tablespoon of cream cheese.
8. Fill the middle of each square with a teaspoon of SPAM filling.
9. Form a triangle out of the dough by folding it in half.
10. Twelve minutes in the oven.

PINEAPPLE FRIED RICE AND SPAM WITH REDUCED SODIUM

INGREDIENTS:
- 2 gently beaten eggs
- split into 1.1/2 teaspoons of salt
- a pinch of freshly ground white pepper
- Divide 1 (12-ounce) can think of SPAM in half and set aside 2 teaspoons of vegetable oil. Sodium-reduced, diced
- 1/2 cup tiny button mushrooms, quartered
- 3 cups of white rice that has been cooked
- light soy sauce (about 2 teaspoons)
- 1/2 cup frozen peas, thawed
- 1 cup fresh pineapple chunks (diced)
- 2 green onions, chopped (including the tips)

INSTRUCTIONS:
1. Whisk together the eggs, 12 tsp salt, and white pepper in a small mixing bowl. One tablespoon of oil in a skillet or wok over high heat, tilting to coat the edges of the pan. In a separate bowl, whisk together the eggs. Cook, constantly stirring, until the sauce is thickened throughout but still wet. Remove the skillet from the heat.
2. Remove the skillet from the oven. Heat the remaining 1 tablespoon of vegetable oil in a skillet, tilting it to cover the sides.

Add chopped SPAM to the mix. Sodium intake is reduced—Stir-fry for 2 to 3 minutes, or until the vegetables are gently browned. Mushrooms should be included. Stir-fry for 1 to 2 minutes, or until the bottom of the pan begins to brown.

3. Toss in the rice—Cook for 2 minutes on high heat. Add in the soy sauce and mix well. Mix well with the eggs, peas, and the remaining 1 teaspoon salt—Stir-fry for 1 to 2 minutes, or until the mixture boils. Combine the pineapple and green onions in a large mixing bowl.

NO DELICIOUS SPAM TERIYAKI

INGREDIENTS:
- 1 can (12 ounces) of SPAM thin pieces of Teriyaki marinated beef
- 1 cup HOUSE OF TSANG TEXTURED WATER Teriyaki Stir-Fry Sauce
- Two cups of stir-fry sauce carrots, peppers, pea pods, bok choy (sliced), and green onions (julienned) are some of the veggies to use.
- 8 ounces of lo mein or linguine noodles, fully cooked

INSTRUCTIONS:
1. Cook the SPAM Teriyaki in a skillet until it is gently browned, then remove it from the pan and put it aside.
2. Cook the veggies in the pan until they are crisp-tender, about 10 minutes.
3. Prepare the noodles according to the package instructions before draining and combining them with the Stir-Fry Sauce.
4. Combine the veggies and noodles in a large mixing bowl until thoroughly blended.
5. Arrange the noodles and top them with the SPAM Teriyaki sauce in individual dishes.

DIP WITH BACON, SPAM, AND CHEESEBURGER

INGREDIENTS:

- 1 (12-ounce) can SPAM with REAL HORMEL Bacon, chopped
- 4 ounces melted cream cheese
- 1 clove of minced garlic
- 1 tablespoon Dijon mustard
- ground beef (around half a pound)
- 1/4 cup mayonnaise
- 1 medium onion, diced (about 1/2 cup)
- a half-cup of sour cream
- mozzarella cheese (about 1/2 cup) shredded
- cheddar cheese (about 1/2 cup shredded)
- ketchup (about 2 tablespoons)
- one-and-a-half tablespoons Worcestershire sauce
- To serve with dipping sauce, use potato or corn chips.

INSTRUCTIONS:

1. Preheat the oven to 350 degrees Fahrenheit.
2. Cook the ground beef thoroughly (to at least 165°F) in a large pan until it is no longer pink, then drain well and set aside.
3. Heat the SPAM with Real HORMEL Bacon in the same skillet until gently browned, then remove from the pan and put aside to cool.
4. Then, in the same pan, sauté the onion and garlic in the drippings until they are translucent.
5. Pour all of the ingredients into a large mixing bowl and stir well. Add the Worcestershire sauce and ketchup and mix well.
6. Add the meat, SPAM, with Real HORMEL Bacon, onions, and garlic in a large mixing bowl until thoroughly blended.

7. Pour the mixture into a baking dish and bake for 15-20 minutes until the mix is hot.
8. Serve with a side of your favorite potato or corn chips to dip into the sauce. This recipe serves 12.

OMELET WITH SPAM (WESTERN OMELET)

INGREDIENTS:
- chopped from 1 (12-ounce) can of SPAM Classic
- 4 teaspoons of butter or margarine
- a quarter teaspoon of chili powder
- 8 big quail eggs
- 1 big green bell pepper, peeled and cut
- 2 medium-sized onions, thinly sliced
- 4 tbsp. of whole milk
- a half teaspoon of salt
- 2 tbsp. vegetable oil

INSTRUCTIONS:
1. Toss the bell pepper and onions in a medium pan with olive oil until they are nicely browned.
2. Stir in the SPAM Classic and chili powder until everything is evenly distributed.
3. Whisk together 2 eggs, 1 tablespoon of milk, 1/8 teaspoon salt, and freshly ground black pepper for each omelet in a large mixing bowl.
4. Melt 1 teaspoon of butter in an omelet pan or skillet with an 8 or 9-inch diameter, and then pour in the egg mixture.
5. Stir constantly over medium heat, gently pushing the cooked edge of the omelet toward the center as the egg sets and tilting the pan to enable the uncooked mixture on one side to flow to the other.

6. To fill the omelet, pour 1/2 cup of the SPAM mixture over half of the omelet, then fold the uncovered half over the filling.
7. Cook until the bottom of the omelet is lightly browned on both sides.

TACOS CON SPAM (SPAM STREET TACOS)

INGREDIENTS:
- SPAM Classic, split into strips from 1 (12-ounce) can
- a quarter teaspoon of ground cumin
- a quarter teaspoon of garlic powder
- a quarter teaspoon of salt and one-quarter teaspoon of chili powder
- a quarter teaspoon of paprika
- a quarter teaspoon of freshly ground black pepper
- a quarter teaspoon of red pepper flakes
- 1 tablespoon extra-virgin olive oil
- 1 (8-ounce) package WHOLLY Guacamole Classic.
- small onion, chopped small Serrano pepper, seeded and chopped 1 small red pepper, sliced
- One taco-sized flour tortilla box (ten tortillas per package).
- Garnish with fresh cilantro, if desired.

INSTRUCTIONS:
1. Put all of the ingredients in a large mixing basin and mix well. Set away. Combine the SPAM Classic, cumin, garlic powder, salt, and pepper.
2. Cook the SPAM Classic until it is lightly browned in a large pan over medium-high heat. Season with salt and pepper and cook for another 1-2 minutes.
3. Fill the tortillas with the SPAM Classic and top with guacamole, onion, and serrano pepper. Garnish with cilantro sprigs, if desired, to finish.

CORNED BEEF AND CABBAGE PANCAKES

INGREDIENTS:
- 1 can (7 ounces) SPAM Classic, coarsely chopped
- corn from a can (8 ounces) cream-style
- 1 big egg (about)
- 1 gallon of milk
- 1 cup of pancake batter
- 1 tablespoon of extra-virgin olive oil

INSTRUCTIONS:
1. Combine the pancake mix, milk, corn, egg, and oil in a medium-sized mixing basin.
2. Add in the SPAM Classic and mix well.
3. Pour the batter onto an oiled griddle, using about a third of a cup for each pancake; cook over medium heat until the bottom is browned, then flip over and brown the other side.
4. Serve pancakes with maple syrup, buttered pancake syrup, or honey on top of the batter.

SLIDERS WITH SPAM AND SAUCY MEATBALLS

INGREDIENTS:
- 12-ounce can of SPAM Classic (for meatballs)
- 1-pound ground beef
- Uncooked bacon (six slices)
- a half-pound of ground pork
- 1 cup toasted breadcrumbs
- 2 quail eggs
- brown sugar (about 2 tablespoons)
- 2 teaspoons ground mustard

- 1 teaspoon of table salt
- Ketchup (two cups) and mustard (one cup)
- 1.1/2 cups granulated sugar
- 1 teaspoon dijon mustard (ground)
- Hawaiian rolls are a kind of bread.

INSTRUCTIONS:

1. Preheat the oven to 350 degrees Fahrenheit.
2. To finely chop the SPAM Classic, bacon, and pork, place all of the ingredients in a food processor and pulse quickly. Do not purée the Ingredients.
3. Combine the mixture with the other meatball ingredients in a large mixing bowl until everything is thoroughly combined.
4. Form the mixture into balls between 1 and 2 inches in diameter with your hands. Place the ingredients in a casserole pan.
5. In a small saucepan, mix all of the sauce ingredients and bring them to a boil over medium heat.
6. Increase heat to high and cook for 2 minutes, often stirring, until water is boiling.
7. Pour the sauce over the meatballs and toss to combine.
8. Preheat the oven to 350°F and bake for 15 minutes. When you bake the meatballs, baste them with the sauce and flip them in the pan. Continue baking for 15 minutes until the internal temperature reaches 165°F, whichever comes first. The dressing should be applied regularly.
9. Serve on buns with pan sauces sprinkled over the top.

ENCHILADAS WITH SPAM

INGREDIENTS:

- 1 can (12 ounces) of SPAM jalapenos, grated,
- 2 tablespoons extra virgin olive oil
- 1 green bell pepper, diced
- 1 big onion, finely chopped
- 1 (15-ounce) can of black beans, drained and rinsed
- 4 cloves garlic, minced
- 1 green bell pepper, diced
- 2 teaspoons finely chopped fresh cilantro
- 2 cups cooked white rice
- split into 2 cups of shredded Mexican mix cheese
- 1 can (about 28 ounces) LA VICTORIA Red Enchilada Sauce
- 8 tortillas (8-inch diameter) made with maize or flour
- To be served with guacamole in its entirety

INSTRUCTIONS:

1. Preheat the oven to 350 degrees Fahrenheit.
2. Allow 1/4 cup of the SPAM mixture to be set aside for garnishing.
3. In a large skillet, heat the oil over medium heat until shimmering.
4. Cook the onion, garlic, and pepper for 5 minutes, or until the onion has cooked, stirring occasionally.
5. Combine everything else (except the garnish) and cook over medium heat for 5 minutes or until it is browned.
6. Stir in the black beans, rice, cilantro, and 1 cup of cheese until everything is well combined before serving.
7. 1/4 cup of the enchilada sauce should be spread over the bottom of a 9-by-13-inch baking dish.
8. Heat the tortillas in a skillet and coat them with enchilada sauce.
9. Spoon the SPAM mixture over each tortilla, then wrap up the tortillas to surround the contents in each.
10. Place each enchilada in a baking dish and pour the remaining enchilada sauce over the tortillas—Bake for 30 minutes at 350°F.
11. The remaining shredded cheese should be sprinkled on top.
12. Cover with aluminum foil and bake for 40-45 minutes, or until the potatoes are heated.

13. If preferred, top with guacamole before serving. Sprinkle the enchiladas with the reserved fried SPAM.

SPAM EGG SALAD SANDWICH SPREAD

INGREDIENTS:
- chopped 1 can (12 ounces) SPAM Classic, finely chopped
- 4 hard-boiled eggs, coarsely chopped
- a third of a cup of mayonnaise
- 1 cup finely chopped celery (2 teaspoons)
- 2 tablespoons pickle relish (sweet or sour)
- 1 teaspoon mustard that has been prepared
- 1 teaspoon of finely chopped onion
- 1 tbsp. table sugar
- season with pepper to taste

INSTRUCTIONS:
1. Combine the SPAM Classic with the other ingredients in a large mixing basin.
2. Refrigerate for at least 1 hour or up to 24 hours after covering with plastic wrap.
3. You may use this spread over your favorite loaf of bread, crackers, or freshly toasted English muffins.

SPAM CRACKLES ON THE ISLANDS OF OAHU

INGREDIENTS:
- 1 can (12 ounces) of SPAM Spicy and a little bit hot
- 45 saltine crackers
- 1 tablespoon of melted butter
- 1 cup brown sugar that has been packed

- butter, salted (two sticks)
- 1 cup coconut flakes or shredded coconut
- 2/3 cup dry roasted macadamia nuts, diced
- 1 cup toasted almonds

INSTRUCTIONS:

1. Prepare an 11-by-17-inch baking pan by lining it with parchment paper.
2. Crackers should be arranged in a single layer on the baking sheet, salt side down.
3. Melt the butter in a pan and cook the shredded SPAM Hot & Spicy till crispy over medium-high heat until the butter has melted.
4. Remove the SPAM Hot & Spicy from the pan and set it on a paper towel to absorb any excess moisture.
5. Combine the brown sugar and 2 sticks of butter in a medium-sized saucepan.
6. Cook, constantly stirring, over medium-low heat until the sugar has completely melted. As soon as the sugar has dissolved, raise the heat to a medium-high setting.
7. Bring the sauce to a boil, constantly stirring, for 2-3 minutes, then pour it over the crackers to coat them.
8. To finish, top with shredded SPAM Hot & Spicy, toasted macadamia nuts, and coconut.
9. Preheat the oven to 350°F and bake for 13 minutes.
10. Allow for 15-20 minutes of cooling time. Separate the crackers into individual crackers. Any leftovers should be stored in the refrigerator.
11. It should be noted that SPAM Classic works excellently in this recipe as well. The number of saltine crackers required is 48 if you use a half-sheet pan (18 inches by 13 inches).

RICE BITES WITH SPICY SPAM

INGREDIENTS:
- 1/4-inch pieces are used. SPAM is a classic.
- 1/4 cup teriyaki sauce
- 3/4 cup white rice that has been cooked
- a tablespoon of HORMEL Real Bacon Bits
- 1 tablespoon furikake (fermented soy sauce)
- 6 drizzles of sriracha mayo dressing
- 2 tablespoons finely chopped green onions

INSTRUCTIONS:
1. Cook the SPAM Classic and teriyaki sauce in a pan until the SPAM Classic is slightly crunchy.
2. Place the SPAM Classic on a dish and let it cool for a few minutes before cutting it into 1.1/2-inch pieces.
3. Cooked rice should be scooped onto each square of SPAM Classic using a tablespoon and smoothed out with a spoon.
4. Furikake and bacon pieces should be equally distributed on top. On top, add some Sriracha Mayonnaise and garnish with green onions. This recipe makes 12 servings.

DONUTS FILLED WITH SPAM

INGREDIENTS:
- Finely chopped SPAM Classic from a 12-ounce can
- 3 tablespoons brown sugar
- 1 (16.3-ounce) can of flaky biscuits from the refrigerator (8 large)
- 1 quart of vegetable oil (for frying purposes)
- 2 cups confectioners' sugar

- Milk (approximately 2-3 teaspoons)

INSTRUCTIONS:

1. 1/4 cup of cubed SPAM Classic should be set aside for the topping.
2. Cook the remaining SPAM Classic in a large pan over medium-high heat until it is browned and crispy on both sides, about 5 minutes. Transfer to a platter and set aside to cool.
3. Cook the 1/4 cup SPAM Classic that has been kept in the same pan with the brown sugar until caramelized and crispy, then put aside to use as a topping.
4. Roll or press each biscuit into a flat circle, one at a time, starting with the largest. Cut off a little circle in the middle using a small cutter to make a doughnut.
5. 1/8 of the SPAM Classic (without the sugar) should be sprinkled on top in a circle around the center of the hole.
6. Fold the biscuit in half and reshape it into a doughnut form. Pinch all sides and the middle to seal the biscuits, and then repeat the process with the remaining biscuits.
7. Preheat the oil in a large cast-iron pan to 325 degrees Fahrenheit. Fry the donuts in batches until they are golden brown, about 2-3 minutes on each side after the oil has reached temperature. Remove the donuts from the pan and place them on a paper towel to drain.
8. Combine powdered sugar and milk in a mixing bowl to make the glaze.
9. Drizzle the donuts with the glaze, and then sprinkle with the brown sugar-coated SPAM Classic on top to finish.
10. Warm the dish before serving. This recipe makes 8 doughnuts. Any leftovers should be stored in the refrigerator.

SPAM SANDWICH ON A PHILLY-DILLY ROLL

INGREDIENTS:

- One can (12 ounces) of SPAM Sodium intake is reduced.
- 1 green bell pepper
- 1 yellow bell pepper
- 1 big yellow onion, peeled and chopped
- 3 tablespoons unsalted butter, cut into quarters
- a total of three tablespoons of Worcestershire sauce is a kind of sauce that comes from the United Kingdom.
- 1/2 to 1 teaspoon freshly ground black pepper, coarsely ground
- 2 loaves of French bread that are thin and slender
- 4 slices of white American cheese, sliced thinly
- 3 pieces of provolone cheese that have been smoked
- 2 tablespoons of dill vegetable dip that has been made

INSTRUCTIONS:

1. Thinly slice the bell peppers and onions to make a salad.
2. Cook them in a large nonstick pan with 2 tablespoons butter over medium-high heat for approximately 10 minutes, until the peppers and onions are soft or until the onions are translucent.
3. To prepare the SPAM Less Sodium, slice it into skinny, non-uniform slices with a sharp knife while the peppers and onions cook on the stovetop.
4. Using tongs, carefully remove the pepper and onion combination from the pan. Set aside and cover with a cloth.
5. Return the skillet to medium-high heat and arrange the SPAM slices in an equal layer on the bottom of the pan.
6. Add the Worcestershire sauce immediately on top of the SPAM slices, coat each piece thoroughly, and then liberally sprinkle with black pepper.
7. Allow for 4 minutes of cooking time before stirring and flipping the SPAM Less Sodium and allowing for another 5 minutes of cooking time, or until the SPAM is cooked through and somewhat crunchy.
8. To toast the bread loaves, slice them almost halfway through and toast them in a separate pan with the remaining butter.

9. She was cooking time: 10 minutes. Return the pepper and onion combination to the pan and cook for another 5 minutes. Add the SPAM Less Sodium Combine all ingredients together, then spread into an equal layer.
10. Reduce the heat to medium and arrange the cheese slices on top of the SPAM mixture in an equal layer. Once the cheese has melted, take the pan from the heat and toss the mixture with a spatula until the cheese is evenly distributed throughout.
11. Place the toasted bread loaves on a serving platter. Apply a skinny coating of the dill dip to the tops of the halves of the bread.
12. The sandwich filling should be scooped onto the bottom half of the bread and sealed. Remove from the oven and slice into appropriate serving sizes to serve immediately.

CAULIFLOWER GRATIN WITH SPAM

INGREDIENTS:
- SPAM Classic, cubed from a 12-ounce can
- all-purpose flour (three tablespoons total)
- butter or margarine (three tablespoons natural)
- Cauliflower, one head (about 1.5 pounds)
- 1 3/4 gallons (liters) of water
- the equivalent of a one-eighth teaspoon of pepper
- 8 tsp. of table salt
- Swiss cheese (1/2 cup) shredded

INSTRUCTIONS:
1. The oven should be preheated to 450 degrees Fahrenheit. A 1.1/2-quart baking dish should be lightly greased.
2. Cauliflower should be cut into tiny florets before cooking. Cook the cauliflower until it's soft in a little quantity of salted boiling water, then drain it well.

3. Whisk the milk into the flour mixture until smooth in a medium saucepan after melting the butter.
4. Pour in the SPAM Classic and cook, constantly stirring, over medium heat until the sauce thickens and boils.
5. In a baking dish, arrange the cauliflower. In a large mixing bowl, combine the SPAM and mayonnaise until thoroughly combined—cheese to finish it off. Depending on how lightly browned you want your bread, this might take 8 to 10 minutes.

QUESADILLAS WITH SPAM

INGREDIENTS:

- 1 can of SPAM (12 ounces) Jalapenos, diced or sliced into thin strips.
- olive oil (around 1 tablespoon)
- red bell pepper (about half a cup chopped)
- half a cup of finely chopped green bell pepper
- 4 tbsp finely chopped yellow onion
- 2 cups finely shredded Mexican mix cheese, split
- 6 (10-inch) tortillas de harina
- cream cheese, 3/4 cup (softened)
- Add sour cream, salsa, guacamole, fresh cilantro, and lime wedges as a finishing touch.

INSTRUCTIONS:

1. After mixing all the salsa ingredients in a medium-sized dish, set aside.
2. Heat the olive oil over medium-high heat until shimmering in a large pan.
3. The onion and bell peppers should be added at this point as well. Cook for 5-8 minutes, or until the vegetables are gently browned and softened, then remove from the pan and place on a plate to cool.

4. In the same pan, heat the SPAM Jalapeo until gently browned, approximately 5 minutes. Remove from heat and set aside.
5. Toss the onions and peppers back into the pan with the SPAM until everything is well combined.
6. Spoon the SPAM-Jalapeo mixture onto the flour tortillas and serve immediately.
7. Serve with salsa and have pleasure in it! In place of the Pineapple Salsa, you may use your favorite prepared fruit or tomato-based salsa if that is what you prefer.

BREAKFAST MUFFINWICH WITH SPAM

INGREDIENTS:
- 1 SPAM Single Classic (Single Spam)
- 2 pieces of sourdough bread
- 1 big egg
- 1 piece of cheddar cheese

INSTRUCTIONS:
1. Heat the SPAM Single in a pan over medium fire until it is golden brown on all sides, then remove from the heat and keep warm.
2. Cook the egg in a separate pan until it reaches the desired doneness.
3. Spread butter on one side of each bread piece to make a sandwich.
4. Place one piece of bread in a pan, butter-side down, then top with SPAM Single, cheese, and a scrambled egg cooked to your liking.
5. Place the bread piece on top of the cheese and toast until golden brown on both sides and the cheese is completely melted. Serve as soon as possible.

SPAM AND NOODLES

INGREDIENTS:
- 1 (12-ounce) can of SPAM with reduced sodium
- 1 (16-ounce) package of dumpling noodles.
- 1 tablespoon of extra-virgin olive oil
- Fresh mushrooms (about 1.1/2 cups sliced)
- 1/3 cup green onions (about 3 tablespoons chopped) Korean Teriyaki Sauce from the HOUSE OF TSANG

INSTRUCTIONS:
1. Bring a pot of water to a boil with salt in it.
2. Cook the dumpling noodles according to the instructions on the box, then drain the noodles.
3. Meanwhile, slice the SPAM Less Sodium into lengths and set it aside.
4. Heat the oil in a large pan over medium-high heat until shimmering.
5. Combine the SPAM Less Sodium, mushrooms, and onions in a large mixing bowl. Five minutes, or until the SPAM Less Sodium is golden brown and the onions and mushrooms are soft, turning regularly, is the time to finish cooking.
6. Toss the vegetables in the pan with the teriyaki sauce until everything is well coated. Combine the noodles and SPAM in a large mixing bowl. Gently toss everything together.

SPAM CARBONARA

INGREDIENTS:
- chopped from 1 (12-ounce) can of SPAM Classic
- 1/4 cup coarsely chopped fresh sage, to taste
- 1 cup frozen green peas (drained)
- 2 teaspoons freshly squeezed lemon juice

- Cooked and drained spaghetti (one 16-ounce bag) as desired
- 1 pinch pepper, or to your liking
- , one-half teaspoon salt-free Mexican or Southwest spice, or your liking
- 3 cups heavy cream (whipped)
- 1/4 cup white wine

INSTRUCTIONS:

1. Heat a sauté pan over medium heat until it is hot.
2. Sauté until the SPAM Classic is faintly golden brown, about 2 minutes.
3. Add the sage and cook for 1 minute or until crispy.
4. Pour wine into the pan to deglaze it. Cook for 2 minutes after stirring in the cream.
5. Cook for 3 minutes, or until the sauce has thickened, after adding the pasta to the pan.
6. Add in the peas and mix well. Season with lemon juice, salt-free seasoning, and freshly ground pepper.

PRETZEL NUGGETS WITH HICKORY SMOKED SPAM

INGREDIENTS:

- cut coarsely, 1 (12-ounce) can SPAM Hickory Smoke
- 2 teaspoons of brown sugar that has been packed
- 1 cup warm milk (110-115 degrees Fahrenheit)
- 3 and a half cups of flour
- One package (about 1/4 ounce) of quick-dry yeast is a kind of yeast that is ready to use immediately.
- mozzarella cheese (about 1/2 cup) shredded
- 1 bunch of finely chopped green onions (about 1 pound)
- quarter-cup finely chopped sun-dried tomatoes
- 4 tablespoons baking soda

- 2-3 tablespoons kosher salt, coarsely ground
- Unsalted butter (four tablespoons) that has been melted

INSTRUCTIONS:

1. Whisk together the brown sugar and heated milk in a small mixing bowl until the sugar is completely dissolved.
2. Whisk together 2.1/2 cups of flour, the milk mixture, and the yeast in a large mixing basin until smooth. Combine all of the ingredients until a soft dough forms.
3. As required, add the remaining flour until the mixture is smooth. Lay a lightly floured area to place the dough and gently knead it for a few minutes, making a softball.
4. Place the dough in a large mixing bowl and cover it with a clean kitchen towel or plastic wrap. Allow the dough to rest in a warm area until it has doubled in size and bubbles begin to develop on the surface of the dough (about 45-60 minutes).
5. The SPAM Hickory Smoke should be chopped and cooked in a pan until gently browned while the dough rises. Set the skillet aside to cool while the dough is rising.
6. Add cheese, green onions, and sun-dried tomatoes to a large mixing bowl once the SPAM Hickory Smoke has been allowed to cool.
7. Turn the dough out onto a lightly floured surface and let it rest for 10 minutes. Divide the mixture into four equal pieces.
8. Flour your hands and rolling pin lightly before beginning. Roll one of the four portions into a rectangle measuring 124 inches long.
9. Filling: Place 1/4 of the SPAM Hickory Smoke mixture down one side of the dough and roll as tightly as possible, beginning with the side that holds the filling and working your way around.
10.]Prepare a baking sheet lined with parchment paper by cutting the chicken into 6-8 (2-inch) pieces and placing them on it (lightly sprayed with nonstick cooking spray).

11. Repeat the process with the remaining three sections of dough. Allow for 20-30 minutes of resting time at room temperature, uncovered.
12. Meanwhile, preheat the oven to 400 degrees Fahrenheit and boil about 6 cups of water. Reduce the heat to a gentle simmer after adding the baking soda.
13. Pretzels should be boiled in batches for approximately 20 seconds and flipped once. The pretzels should have a tiny fluff to them. Transfer the baked goods back to the baking sheets using a slotted spoon. Bake for 12-15 minutes until the puff pastry is golden brown.
14. Warm pretzel nibbles are brushed with melted butter and gently sprinkled with salt. Warm the dish before serving. This recipe makes around 2-3 dozen servings.

PIGGIES ON A BLANKET MADE WITH HAWAIIAN SPAM

INGREDIENTS:

- 1 (12-ounce) can SPAM Classic (or similar)
- 1 (3-ounce) package of cream cheese that has been softened
- Drain 1 can of pineapple tidbits (8 ounces), and set aside
- 1 teaspoon dijon mustard (honey mustard)
- 1 can of crescent roll dough (from the refrigerator)

INSTRUCTIONS:

1. Preheat the oven to 350 degrees Fahrenheit.
2. SPAM Classic should be cut into eight equal pieces.
3. Add the cream cheese, pineapple, and mustard; thoroughly blend.
4. Separate the dough and roll it out on a baking sheet. One slice of SPAM Classic should be placed on the big end of each roll.

5. Roll up the SPAM Classic after spreading it with the cream cheese mixture.
6. Cook for 20 minutes, or until the top is golden brown.

REUBEN'S SPAM ROLL-UPS

INGREDIENTS:
- Finely chopped 1 (12-ounce) can SPAM Classic
- One cup of Thousand Island dressing.
- 1 (14-ounce) can make thoroughly drained sauerkraut
- 2 cups shredded Swiss cheese (or other similar cheese)
- 16-18 pieces of rye bread with swirls in it
- 1/4 cup melted butter (about)

INSTRUCTIONS:
1. Combine the SPAM Classic, the dressing, the sauerkraut, and the cheese in a large mixing bowl; leave aside.
2. Each piece of bread should have the crust removed. With the use of a rolling pin, thinly slice the bread.
3. Spread the SPAM mixture over the bread pieces (about 3 tablespoons) using a spoon. Roll each roll up and cut each roll in half, then brush with melted butter to finish.
4. Place the roll-ups on a baking sheet and bake for 15 minutes. Fifteen minutes at 375 degrees Fahrenheit. This recipe makes 32-36 roll-ups.

HASH WITH SPAM, PUMPKIN SPICE, AND FALL VEGETABLES

INGREDIENTS:

- 2 tablespoons extra-virgin olive oil
- 1 red onion, peeled and chopped
- 1 medium-sized sweet potato, peeled and chopped
- 3 tablespoons pumpkin pie spice (12-ounce can) chopped
- Brussels sprouts (1/4 pound, cut and quartered), about 1 cup
- 1 apple, peeled, cored, and sliced into cubes
- 1/2 tsp. freshly cracked black pepper, to taste
- If desired, 4 fried eggs may be added.

INSTRUCTIONS:

1. Heat the oil in a large cast-iron pan over medium-high heat until shimmering.
2. Cook for 3 minutes, or until the onions are transparent.
3. Cook for 7 to 10 minutes until the sweet potatoes are golden brown.
4. Combine the SPAM Pumpkin Spice, Brussels sprouts, and apple in a large mixing bowl.
5. Stir often for 5 to 6 minutes, or until well cooked and nicely browned.
6. Season with freshly ground pepper. If desired, top with scrambled eggs.

GRILLED CHEESE WITH SPAM, PUMPKIN SPICE, AND CHEDDAR

INGREDIENTS:

- Cut one (12-ounce) can of pumpkin spice can into eight pieces.
- 1/4 cup melted butter or margarine, preferably softened
- 8 slices of country-style bread (1/2-inch thick)
- thinly sliced 8 ounces of shredded white cheddar cheese
- 1 medium yellow onion, caramelized
- 1 Granny Smith apple, which I half before coring and cutting it.

INSTRUCTIONS:

1. Cook the SPAM Pumpkin Spice slices in a large pan over medium-high heat for 3 to 5 minutes, or until they are browned.
2. Half of the cheese should be distributed equally across four pieces of bread. Combine SPAM Pumpkin Spice with caramelized onion and apple pieces, then top with the remaining cheese.
3. Cover with the remainder of the bread pieces. Butter, both sides of each sandwich, using a pastry brush.
4. Sandwiches should be cooked on a grill or in a large nonstick pan over medium heat, flipping once, for 5 to 6 minutes, or until golden brown on both sides and the cheese has melted.

BREAD PUDDING WITH HAWAIIAN SPAM

INGREDIENTS:

- One can (12 ounces) of SPAM Sodium intake is reduced. 1.1/3 cups packed light brown sugar, divided 2 (4.4-ounce) packages sweet dinner rolls, broken into cubes 5 tablespoons melted butter, divided 1.1/3 cups packed light brown sugar, split
- 1 fresh pineapple, peeled, cored, and cut into slices, ripe but not overripe
- 3 cups heavy whipping cream 5 eggs, beaten
- 1.1/4 cups sugar (split into quarters)
- 1 teaspoon pure vanilla extract
- 1 cup gently toasted sliced almonds, melted in 1/2 cup softened butter

INSTRUCTIONS:

1. Preheat the oven to 350 degrees Fahrenheit.
2. Prepare a 9 x 13-inch baking dish with cooking spray.
3. Cook SPAM Less Sodium in 2 tablespoons of butter and 1/3 cup of brown sugar in a big pan until gently cooked, about 3 minutes total.

4. Arrange the bread cubes, SPAM product, and pineapple on a serving plate. The remaining 3 tablespoons of melted butter should be drizzled over the top.
5. In a medium-sized mixing basin, whisk together the eggs, cream, 1 cup granulated sugar, and vanilla extract until well blended.
6. Pour the egg mixture over the bread mixture and softly push down with a fork until the bread is completely coated with the mixture.
7. Bake for 45 minutes or until the middle is firm to the touch.
8. Between now and then, in a medium-sized mixing basin, combine softened butter, the remaining 1 cup brown sugar, the remaining 1/4 cup sugar, and the almonds until the mixture is well combined.
9. Spread or press the mixture onto a baking pan lined with parchment paper.
10. Bake for 15 minutes until the mixture is bubbling and golden; remove from the oven and set aside to cool completely. Break up the mixture into small pieces. Sprinkle the topping on top of the pudding.

ORIGINAL BAKED SPAM

INGREDIENTS:

- 1 (12-ounce) can SPAM Classic (or similar)
- 10 whole cloves of garlic
- a third cup of brown sugar that has been packed
- 1 teaspoon water
- 1 teaspoon mustard
- 1 teaspoon vinegar
- a half teaspoon of vinegar

INSTRUCTIONS:

1. Preheat the oven to 375 degrees Fahrenheit. Placing SPAM Classic on a rack in a small baking pan is a good idea. The surface should be scored, and cloves should be inserted.
2. Brown sugar, water, mustard, and vinegar are combined in a mixing basin and stirred until smooth. Using a pastry brush, glaze the SPAM loaf. Bake for 20 minutes, basting occasionally. Prepare to serve by slicing.

BURRITO MUSUBI

INGREDIENTS:

- 1 can (12 ounces) of SPAM Traditionally prepared and split into strips
- 1/4 cup of all-purpose flour
- 2 eggs, lightly beaten
- 1 cup panko breadcrumbs
- Vegetable oil is a kind of oil that comes from plants.
- 8 sheets of nori seaweed
- 3 cups sushi rice that has been cooked
- Furikake
- scrambled eggs for four people
- 1 cup of coleslaw dressing
- 1/2 cup French fried onions, julienned
- 1 small cucumber, julienned
- Unagi sauce

INSTRUCTIONS:

1. Prepare three shallow plates by separating the flour, eggs, and breadcrumbs.
2. Dip the SPAM Classic strips in flour, eggs, and breadcrumbs until they are well coated.
3. Add enough vegetable oil to cover the bottom by 1 inch in a large pan and heat over medium-high heat until the vegetable oil is hot.

4. Fry the breaded SPAM Classic strips in a pan for 3 to 5 minutes, flipping once until they are browned on both sides. Remove the skillet from the heat.
5. One sheet of nori should be placed in the work area. Rice should be distributed uniformly over the nori using damp hands, leaving a 3/4 inch strip of nori exposed on one end. Furikake should be sprinkled on top of the rice.
6. Stack fried SPAM Classic strips, eggs, coleslaw mix, cucumber, and French-fried onions on a nori sheet, then sprinkle with Unagi sauce and wrap up. Repeat the process with the remaining components.

MUSUBI WITH KIMCHI FRIED RICE

INGREDIENTS:

- 2 tbsp soy sauce
- 1 cup sugar (or 2 teaspoons)
- 1 (12-ounce) can SPAM Classic, sliced into 8 halves
- 1 teaspoon extra-virgin olive oil
- a half cup of diced kimchi
- 1 tablespoon gochujang paste (Chinese chili paste)
- 3 cups sushi rice that has been cooked
- 1 cup finely sliced green onions
- 1 teaspoon sesame oil
- 1 teaspoon sesame seeds
- 1.1/2 cups cucumber slices (about)
- 4 nori sheets, each half-sheeted

INSTRUCTIONS:

1. Soy sauce and sugar should be combined in a small bowl.
2. Cook the SPAM Classic slices in a large pan over medium-high heat for 3 to 5 minutes, or until they are browned. Cook for 1 to 2 minutes until the pieces are coated with the soy sauce sugar

mixture. Remove from the pan and use a paper towel to clean the skillet.

3. Heat the oil over medium heat in the same big skillet until shimmering. Stir in the kimchi and gochujang paste for 1 to 2 minutes, or until everything is well blended. Stir in the rice, sesame oil, sesame seeds, and green onions for 1 to 2 minutes, or until everything is well mixed. Remove the pan from the heat.

4. Place a third cup of rice in a musubi press, or a plastic-lined SPAM can on top of a divided nori sheet and press down to compact the rice. Take away the press. Place cucumber slices on a bed of rice and top with a piece of SPAM Classic. Wrap each nori sheet in a single layer. To attach the two ends, moisten one end gently with water.

LONO AMERICAN MUSUBI

INGREDIENTS:

- 2 slices each of 1 (12-ounce) can of SPAM Classic
- 3 cups sushi rice that has been cooked
- 4 nori sheets, sliced in half, with Secret Sauce
- 2 yellow onions, caramelized in a skillet
- 2 cups of finely shredded lettuce
- Secret Sauce
- 1/2 cup mayonnaise
- ketchup (three tablespoons)
- finely chopped white onion (about 2 tablespoons)
- 1.1/2 tablespoons coarsely chopped dill pickle relish
- 1.1/2 teaspoons ground cumin
- 3/4 teaspoon sugar
- 1/4 teaspoon mustard (yellow)
- 1/8 teaspoon of table salt

INSTRUCTIONS:

1. Cook the SPAM Classic in a large pan over medium-high heat for 3 to 5 minutes, or until it is browned. Remove the skillet from the heat.
2. Insert nori sheet halves into the center of the musubi press or plastic-lined SPAM Classic can and press down. Repeat with remaining rice until all of the nori sheet halves are used. Drizzle with Secret Sauce and serve immediately. Add caramelized onions, lettuce, a SPAM piece, and two halves of the cheese slices on top.
3. Wrap each nori sheet in a single layer. To attach the two ends, moisten one end gently with water. Make another eight by repeating the process.

Secret Sauce

1. Combine the ingredients in a small mixing dish.

HAWAIIAN LOCAL BURGER

INGREDIENTS:

TO MAKE PINEAPPLE SOY GLAZE:

- 3 cups granulated sugar
- 2 quarts of soy sauce
- 2 cups pineapple chunks (crushed)
- garlic, minced (about 2 teaspoons)
- 2 tbsp lime juice
- hoisin sauce (about 4 tablespoons)

IN THE CASE OF THE SLIDER:

- 1/4 inch-thick slices of fried SPAM Classic, cooked till crispy
- 1 sweet Hawaiian dinner roll (about)
- Green onions that have been finely sliced
- with a pineapple-soy glaze on top, 1 (16 ounces) ground beef patty

INSTRUCTIONS:

1. To prepare the pineapple soy glaze, combine the brown sugar, soy sauce, pineapple, garlic, lime juice, and hoisin sauce in a saucepan over medium-high heat until the sugar is completely dissolved. Simmer until the glaze has thickened, then turn off the heat and let it cool completely on a rack.
2. To create the sliders, heat a separate skillet over medium heat, cook the SPAM Classic until golden brown, and then remove it from the pan.
3. Form the meat into 2-ounce patties by rolling and flattening it.
4. Cook the tiny patties until they reach an internal temperature of 160°F at the very least (use a calibrated handheld thermometer to verify the cooking temperature).
5. After the hamburger has been cooked, drizzle 2 tablespoons of glaze over it.
6. The Assembly of the slider begins with dividing the dinner roll in half and putting the beef patty on the bottom slice of the registration.
7. The SPAM Classic is American and stacked on top of the beef patty, drizzled with more glaze, and garnished with green onions.
8. Place the top of the dinner roll on top of the stack and serve immediately.

BAKED BEANS

INGREDIENTS:

- 12-ounce can SPAM Classic (cut into cubes), drained and rinsed
- butter or margarine (around 1 tablespoon)
- chile powder (half a teaspoon)
- 1 tablespoon chili sauce
- 1 tablespoon molasses
- 2 medium-sized onions, roughly chopped
- TWO (15-ounce) cans of vegetarian kidney beans in tomato sauce

INSTRUCTIONS:
1. Preheat the oven to 400 degrees Fahrenheit.
2. Prepare a 1.1/2-quart baking dish with cooking spray.
3. Melt the butter in a medium pan over medium-high heat until it begins to foam.
4. Sauté for 5 to 6 minutes, or until the onions have become translucent.
5. Combine the onions, beans, chili sauce, molasses, and chili powder in a large baking dish, stirring well after each addition.
6. Cover with a lid after stirring in SPAM Classic.
7. Bake for 30 to 35 minutes, stirring regularly, or until the mixture is heated and the flavors are mixed.

HUEVOS CHILAQUILES (CHILAQUILES EGGS)

INGREDIENTS:
- 12-ounce can of SPAM Classic, sliced into small pieces
- Four cups of corn tortilla chips.
- 12 cups CHI-CHI'S Thick & Chunky Hot Salsa
- cheese shredded Chihuahua cheese or Monterey Jack cheese (to taste)
- a total of four fried eggs

INSTRUCTIONS:
1. Cook the SPAM Classic strips in a large pan over medium-high heat for 3 to 5 minutes until they are browned and crisped.
2. Preheat the oven to 350 degrees Fahrenheit. Prepare a 13-by-nine-inch baking dish by lightly greasing it.
3. Half of the tortilla chips should be placed in the baking dish that has been prepared. Half of the cooked SPAM Classic strips, half of the salsa, and 1 cup of cheese should be placed on top. Gently press the layers into the casserole dish. Continue with the

remaining tortilla chips, SPAM Classic strips, salsa, and cheese until all ingredients are used.
4. Bake for 30 minutes until the cheese melts, and the top is golden brown. One egg is placed on top of each dish.

MACARONI AND CHEESE BAKE

INGREDIENTS:
- chopped from 1 (12-ounce) can of SPAM Classic
- all-purpose flour (about 1 tablespoon)
- butter or margarine, split into two teaspoons
- 1/4 teaspoon dry mustard
- 8 ounces elbow macaroni with cheese
- a half-cup of freshly made breadcrumbs (1 slice)
- 1 tsp. freshly ground red pepper (cayenne)
- 2 quarts of milk
- a quarter teaspoon of paprika
- pasteurized sharp American cheese, diced (about 1/2 pound)
- a quarter teaspoon of salt

INSTRUCTIONS:
1. Preheat the oven to 400 degrees Fahrenheit.
2. Prepare a 2-quart casserole pan by lightly greasing it.
3. Cook the macaroni according to the instructions on the box, then drain.
4. Toss the SPAM Classic and macaroni together in a casserole dish.
5. One tablespoon of butter should be melted in a medium pot. Mix in the flour, salt, mustard, black pepper, and cayenne until the mixture is smooth.
6. Cook, constantly stirring, over medium heat, until the sauce thickens and boils for about 10 minutes. Cook, constantly stirring, until the cheese is completely melted.
7. Pour the sauce over the SPAM mixture and combine well.
8. Melt the remaining 1 tablespoon of butter in a microwave-safe bowl, then toss the breadcrumbs and paprika until well combined.

9. Sprinkle on top of the macaroni. Preheat the oven to 200°F and bake for 20-25 minutes.

BACON SPAM AND POTATO PANCAKES

INGREDIENTS:
- 4 cups mashed potatoes (or equivalent)
- Fully cooked luncheon meat with bacon (such as SPAM with Bacon) in a 12-ounce can, diced
- pancake mix (with buttermilk) 1 cup
- 2 gently beaten eggs
- 2 tbsp. vegetable oil

INSTRUCTIONS:
1. Gradually combine the mashed potatoes, luncheon meat, pancake mix, and eggs in a large mixing basin.
2. In a skillet, heat the oil over medium heat until shimmering. Spoon the potato mixture into the heated oil and flatten it with a spatula to make it uniform in thickness—Cook for 3 to 5 minutes, or until the bottom is crispy. Flip the pan over and cook for another 3 to 4 minutes until the second side is brown and crispy.

BURGERS WITH SPAM

INGREDIENTS:
- Thoroughly cooked luncheon meat (such as SPAM) in a 12-ounce can, coarsely chopped
- One large hard-boiled egg, peeled and diced.
- Shred 1 box (8 ounces) of celery. Cheddar cheese is a kind of cheese.
- 1/2 cup coarsely chopped onion
- 1/2 cup mayonnaise
- 1/4 cup chili sauce

- *1/2-tablespoon salt*
- *1/4-tablespoon spicy sauce*
- *12 hamburger buns, cut in half*

INSTRUCTIONS:
1. Preheat the broiler by positioning an oven rack about 6 inches from the heat source.
2. Combine the luncheon meat, eggs, Cheddar cheese, and onion in a large mixing bowl. Combine the mayonnaise, chili sauce, salt, and spicy sauce in a mixing bowl. Make a thorough mix.
3. Spread the meat mixture on the insides of the hamburger bread halves. Place on a baking sheet and bake for 20 minutes.
4. Cook under the broiler in the preheated oven for 5 to 10 minutes, or until the cheese is golden and bubbling.

CUPCAKES WITH SPAM-A-LICIOUS FROSTING AND SALTED CARAMEL GLAZE

INGREDIENTS:
- *1 (15.25 ounce) packet of devil's food cake mix*
- *4 ounces thoroughly cooked luncheon meat (such as SPAM), shredded 1 (15.25 ounce) container vanilla pudding mix*
- *1.1/3 glasses of water*
- *1 cup prepared mayonnaise*
- *2 giant eggs (about)*
- *Frosting:*
- *1/2 cup melted butter*
- *1 cup molasses (or dark brown sugar)*
- *1/3 cup heavy whipping cream*

- *1 / 4 teaspoon of salt*

- *\2 cups confectioners' sugar, or as much as you need*

INSTRUCTIONS:

1. Preheat the oven to 350 degrees Fahrenheit (175 degrees C). Prepare 24 muffin cups by greasing them or lining them with paper muffin liners.
2. Using a large skillet, cook the ingredients over medium-high heat. Cook and stir the grated luncheon meat in a heated pan until it is browned and crispy for 5 to 7 minutes. Transfer the heart to a dish lined with paper towels and allow it to cool fully.
3. In a large mixing bowl, using an electric mixer on low speed, combine the cake mix, water, mayonnaise, and eggs until barely moistened, about 2 minutes. Increase the speed to medium and beat until the mixture is smooth, approximately 2 minutes. 2/3 of the fried luncheon meat should be folded into the cake batter. Pour the batter into the muffin cups that have been prepared.
4. Bake in the oven for approximately 20 minutes or until a toothpick inserted into the middle of a cupcake comes out clean. Allow cooling in the pans, which should be placed on wire racks.
5. Melt the butter in a small saucepan over medium heat, stirring constantly. Stir in the brown sugar and heavy cream until the sugar is completely dissolved. Bring the sauce to a simmer and let it cook for 1 minute without stirring. Remove the pan from the heat, mix in the salt, and allow the sauce to cool thoroughly.
6. To make the frosting, transfer the sauce to a large mixing bowl and gradually add confectioners' sugar, 1 cup at a time, until it achieves the required consistency. Spread the leftover fried luncheon meat on top of the cupcakes once they have been allowed to cool.

SPAM SANDWICHES ON THE BARBECUE

INGREDIENTS:

- completely prepared luncheon meat in a 12-ounce container (e.g., Spam)

- *1 and a half cups of barbecue sauce*
- *1 cup of coleslaw that has been prepared*
- *2 slices 1 loaf of French bread, divided and toasted*
- *1 loaf of French bread, sliced into 4 pieces*

INSTRUCTIONS:
1. *Thinly slice the lunch meat to serve as sandwiches. In a large pan, cook the sliced lunch meat and barbeque sauce over medium heat until the meat is heated. Continue to cook until well heated. Place the meat and spice on the bottom half of the toasted bread and toast until golden brown. Place the coleslaw on top, followed by the other half of the slices of bread.*

SPAM AND BACON, MAKING DEVILED EGGS

INGREDIENTS:
- *6 giant eggs (about)*
- *3 tablespoons mayonnaise*
- *SPAM with bacon, coarsely chopped (about 3 ounces)*
- *1/2 cup finely chopped fresh dill pickle*
- *1 tablespoon yellow mustard that has been prepared*
- *a quarter teaspoon of salt*
- *1 pinch paprika, to be used as a garnish*

INSTRUCTIONS:
1. *Place the eggs in a single layer in a pot and fill with water to cover the eggs plus one inch on both sides. Bring the water to a boil, then cover and turn off the heat. Allow for 15 minutes of resting time.*
2. *Transfer the eggs to a cold water bath as soon as possible to expedite chilling. Eggs should be tapped on a flat surface to break the shell and peel them.*

3. Cut the eggs in half lengthwise and put the yolks aside in a small basin while preparing the whites.
4. With a fork, mash the yolks and mayonnaise together; toss the SPAM with the bacon, pickle, mustard, and salt. Fill the egg whites with the yolk mixture. Paprika may be used as a garnish if desired.

SPAM MUSUBI

INGREDIENTS:
- 2 cups short-grain white rice (uncooked), drained
- 2 quarts of water
- 1 cup rice vinegar (about 6 teaspoons)
- 1/4 cup soy sauce
- 1/4 cup oyster sauce (about)
- 1/2 cup granulated sugar
- completely prepared luncheon meat in a 12-ounce container (e.g., Spam)
- 5 sheets of nori (sushi rice) (dry seaweed)
- 2 tbsp. vegetable oil

INSTRUCTIONS:
1. Uncooked rice should be soaked for 4 hours before draining and rinsing.
2. Two cups of water should be brought to a boil in a saucepan. Stir in the rice until it is evenly distributed. Reduce the heat to low, cover, and cook for 20 minutes. Remove the pan from the heat and put it aside to cool.
3. Combine soy sauce, oyster sauce, and sugar in a separate mixing bowl until thoroughly dissolved. Remove from heat and set aside. Luncheon meat should be sliced lengthwise into 10 slices or to desired thickness and marinated in the sauce for 5 minutes before serving. ***
4. In a large skillet, heat the oil over medium-high heat until shimmering—Cook the slices for 2 minutes on each side, or until they are gently browned on both sides. Nori sheets should be cut

and laid down on a level work area. Push the rice into the middle of each sheet using a rice press until it is completely sealed. Remove the media from the top and top it with a piece of luncheon meat. Wrap the nori around the rice mold, pressing the edges with a bit of water to seal. (Alternatively, rice may be molded by hand into the shape of meat slices that are 1 inch thick.) Musubi may be served either hot or cold, depending on your preference.

SPAM FRIED RICE

INGREDIENTS:
- 1 (12-ounce) can of fully cooked luncheon meat (such as SPAM), cut into small cubes
- Sesame oil (around a tablespoon)
- 1 medium-sized onion, chopped
- 4 cups cooked rice that has been left over
- 1 cup peas and carrots from the freezer
- 4 giant eggs that have been beaten
- 2 tbsp soy sauce
- 12 tablespoons of Sriracha sauce
- 4 big quail eggs
- season with salt and freshly ground black pepper to taste
- 1 tablespoon shredded nori (or more to your liking)
- 1 tablespoon thinly sliced onions, or more to your liking
- 1 teaspoon sesame seeds, or to your preference
- 1 teaspoon black sesame seeds, or more to your liking

INSTRUCTIONS:
1. Using a large skillet, cook the ingredients over medium-high heat. Fry the Spam for 5 to 7 minutes, or until it is gently browned. Place on a serving dish.
2. In the same pan, heat sesame oil over medium heat until shimmering, approximately 1 minute. Add the onion and cook, occasionally stirring, until it softens, about 5 minutes. Reduce the heat to low and stir in the rice and frozen veggies, cooking until

the rice is cooked, approximately 5 minutes. In a large mixing bowl, combine the rice and the beaten eggs. Stir until curds form, about 3 to 4 minutes. Remove the rice mixture from the pan and set it aside.
3. Half of the Spam should be returned to the pan, and the eggs should be mixed with the remaining rice mixture. Toss in the soy sauce and Sriracha. Remove the pan from the heat after mixing.
4. Pour the remaining eggs into a pan over medium heat and cook until set. Cook for about 1 minute, or until the outside edges are opaque. Cook until the whites are fully set, approximately 4 minutes, then remove the lid and decrease the heat to low—season with salt and freshly ground pepper.
5. On top of the fried rice, arrange the fried eggs and Spam (reserved), then garnish with nori, scallions, and sesame seeds, to taste.

TACOS DE SPAM

INGREDIENTS:
- 1 can (12 ounces) of light luncheon meat (such as Spam)
- sprayed on frying spray
- 12 (1.25 ounce) packets of taco spice mix, or more according to personal preference
- 2 teaspoons water, or as much as you need
- 8 flour tortillas (6 inches in diameter)
- 8 ounces of finely chopped lettuce
- 7 to 8 ounces of shredded Cheddar cheese
- Drained and cut olives from 2 (2.25 ounce) cans (2.25 pounds)
- 1 medium-sized tomato, diced
- 1 medium-sized onion, diced

INSTRUCTIONS:
1. Using a cheese grater, shred luncheon meat onto a big platter and set it aside.
2. Cook over medium-high heat in a large skillet sprayed with cooking spray until hot. Add the shredded luncheon meat and

heat, constantly stirring, until it starts to brown, about 5 minutes. Combine taco seasoning and water in a large mixing bowl. Cook, constantly stirring, for 5 to 7 minutes, or until the luncheon meat is uniformly seasoned and lightly browned. Reduce the heat to a low setting to stay warm.
3. Another skillet should be sprayed with cooking spray and heated over medium-high heat. Place 1 tortilla in the skillet and cook until cooked through, approximately 30 seconds on each side, until the tortilla is crisp and golden. Repeat the process with the remaining tortillas.
4. Warm tortillas should be topped with luncheon meat, lettuce, Cheddar cheese, olives, tomato, and onion before serving.

TACOS WITH SPAM SHREDDED

INGREDIENTS:
- cooking spray
- Canned luncheon meat with minimal sodium, one (12-ounce) can (such as SPAM)
- 12 (1-ounce) packages of taco seasoning mix.
- 2 tablespoons water, or more if necessary
- 1 flour tortilla (8 inches in diameter)
- 1 package (8 ounces) of shredded iceberg lettuce
- 8 ounces of solid block cheese, shredded Cheddar cheese
- 1 small onion, diced
- 2 (2.5 ounces) can slice black olives, drained
- 1 small tomato, diced

INSTRUCTIONS:
1. Cook the luncheon meat in a large pan sprayed with cooking spray over medium-high heat until it is browned. Cook for approximately 5 minutes, stirring constantly, or until the sauce is gently caramelized. Stir in the taco seasoning mix until it is evenly distributed. Pour in the water and simmer, constantly stirring, for 2 to 3 minutes, or until the water evaporates

completely. Reduce the heat to a low setting to keep the luncheon meat warm.
2. Cook 1 tortilla until cooked through in a separate pan, approximately 1 minute on each side, sprayed with cooking spray, and placed over medium-high heat; repeat with remaining tortillas. Repeat the process with the remaining tortillas.
3. Salad meat, lettuce, Cheddar cheese, tomato, onion, and black olives should be layered onto each tortilla before rolling it up.

SANDWICHES WITH HAM AND CHEESE (PA-SPAM-MI)

INGREDIENTS:
- 12-ounce can of SPAM with Bacon
- 1/2 teaspoon ground coriander
- 1/4 cup prepared yellow mustard
- 1 teaspoon ground cumin
- 2 French baguettes
- 4 slices provolone cheese.

INSTRUCTIONS:
1. Preheat the oven to 375 degrees Fahrenheit (190 degrees C).
2. Using the big holes on a cheese grater, shred SPAM until it is finely chopped.
3. Fry the shredded SPAM and coriander in a large pan over medium-high heat until the SPAM is browned, about 5 minutes.
4. On the bottom half of each French roll, spread 1 tablespoon of yellow mustard, then top each with 2 slices of provolone cheese. Place the rolls on a baking pan and bake for 15 minutes at 350 degrees.
5. Bake for approximately 5 minutes or until the cheese has melted.
6. Cooked SPAM should be divided between the buns, folded, and served immediately.

SPAM-OCADO HASH

INGREDIENTS:
- 12-ounce can SPAM with Bacon (cut into 1/2-inch pieces), drained
- 1 teaspoon vegetable oil, or as required, for frying
- 1 delicious yellow onion, peeled and sliced into wedges
- Peeled and pitted avocados (cut into 1-inch cubes): 2 avocados
- 4 giant eggs, seasoned with salt and freshly ground black pepper to taste
- 1 lime, freshly squeezed or to taste

INSTRUCTIONS:
1. Prepare SPAM and Bacon in a large pan over medium heat, constantly stirring, until barely browned, approximately 7 minutes; remove from skillet and leave away to cool.
2. Add enough oil to cover the bottom of the same pan; cook and toss the onion and avocado until browned, approximately 7 minutes; remove from heat.
3. A nonstick pan over medium heat should be preheated; break the eggs into the skillet and cook until the whites are mostly set, approximately 2 minutes. Eggs should be gently flipped and cooked until the desired doneness is attained, roughly 2 minutes for over-easy eggs; season with salt and pepper to taste.
4. Stir the SPAM and bacon back into the pan with the onion mixture, then sprinkle with lime juice on top.
5. Make four servings of hash by dividing it among four dishes and placing an egg on top.

THE SPAM ON THE MOVE

INGREDIENTS:
- 2 packages (8 ounces each) of uncooked spaghetti
- 1 tablespoon of extra-virgin olive oil

- Fully cooked luncheon meat (such as Spam) in a 12-ounce jar with diced green onions, garlic, and one tablespoon of soy sauce.
- 1/2 cup of water
- 12 tablespoons sesame oil
- freshly ground black pepper (about 1 teaspoon)

INSTRUCTIONS:
1. Bring a big saucepan of lightly salted water to a boil, then reduce the heat to low—Cook the pasta for 8 to 10 minutes, or until it is al dente, before draining.
2. Meanwhile, heat the vegetable oil in a medium skillet over medium heat until shimmering. Sauté the luncheon meat, green onion, and garlic until the meat is lightly browned. Cooked spaghetti is added last, followed by soy sauce, water, sesame oil, and pepper to taste. Combine all of the ingredients, heat through, and serve.

SPAM AND POTATO SOUP

INGREDIENTS:
- 6 baked potatoes (medium size)
- SPAM Classic or another kind (12-ounce can), cut into cubes
- 5 tbsp. butter
- 5 tbsp. all-purpose flour
- 4 quarts of milk
- Taste for seasoning with 1/2 teaspoon salt and freshly ground black pepper.
- cheese (about 1 cup shredded Cheddar)

INSTRUCTIONS:
1. Preheat the oven to 450 degrees Fahrenheit (230 degrees C). Make many fork pricks in the potatoes before putting them on a baking pan to bake.
2. Bake in the preheated oven for 50 to 1 hour, or until potatoes are readily penetrated with a fork until potatoes are tender. When

the potatoes have cooled enough to handle, scoop off the flesh and mash it softly with a knife in a large mixing basin.
3. Using a pan over medium heat, cook and stir SPAM Classic until it browns.
4. Melt the butter in a large saucepan over medium-low heat, stirring until the batter is smooth. Cook, constantly stirring, until the roux is thoroughly mixed and bubbling; then add the milk—season with salt and freshly ground pepper.
5. 5 minutes. Stir in potatoes and SPAM Classic and simmer until potatoes are cooked, approximately 5 minutes longer than the actual cooking time.
6. Serve in individual bowls, with roughly 1/4 cup of Cheddar cheese on top of each serving.

SPAM, RED BEANS, AND RICE

INGREDIENTS:
- 3 cups uncooked white rice, drained and rinsed
- 3 quarts of water
- Cubed thoroughly cooked luncheon meat (such as SPAM) 1 (12 ounces) can of kidney beans with liquid 3 (15 ounces) cans of kidney beans without liquid
- 1/4 cup melted butter
- 18 teaspoon dried onion flakes

INSTRUCTIONS:
1. Cook the rice and water in a saucepan over high heat until the rice is tender. Reduce the heat to medium-low, cover, and cook for 20 to 25 minutes until the rice is cooked and the liquid has been absorbed, whichever comes first.
2. In a large saucepan, combine the luncheon meat and kidney beans with liquid, butter, and onion flakes until everything is well combined. Bring medium-high heat to a simmer, then lower the heat to medium-low, cover, and continue to cook for 15

minutes, stirring regularly. To serve, spoon the beans over the hot rice and sprinkle with salt and pepper.

SPAM MUSUBI

INGREDIENTS:
- 1/2 cup granulated sugar
- 1/4 cup light soy sauce
- 1/4 cup oyster sauce (about)
- 2- 12-ounce cans of low-sodium canned luncheon meat (for example, SPAM), cut into 1/2-inch pieces.
- 2 and a half cups of water
- 2 cups medium-grain white rice (about) (such as Calrose)
- 1 cup rice vinegar (about 6 teaspoons)
- Seaweed, divided into 1.1/2-inch pieces, from 1 (1.2 ounces) container of roasted and seasoned seaweed

INSTRUCTIONS:
1. Combine the sugar, soy sauce, and oyster sauce in a gallon-size resealable bag and set aside. Add the luncheon meat to the bag and close it. Turn the bag to coat the luncheon meat, gently pressing the bag to coat the meat. Allow for at least 1 hour of marinating time.
2. Bring a pot of water to a boil, then add the rice. Bring the water back to a spot, decrease the heat to low, and continue to cook until the liquid has been absorbed and the rice is cooked, approximately 15 minutes.
3. Cook the luncheon meat and marinade in a pan over medium-high heat until the meat is cooked through. Cook for approximately 5 minutes, turning often, or until the luncheon meat is browned and the marinade has been absorbed.
4. Stir in the rice vinegar until everything is well-combined.
5. Mix the rice and seaweed in a large mixing bowl; add the luncheon meat and mix well.

BURGERS MADE WITH SPAM

INGREDIENTS:
- completely prepared luncheon meat in a 12-ounce container (e.g., Spam)
- 4 hard-boiled eggs
- 4 fluid ounces of cheese, cubed
- 1 big onion, diced
- 3 tablespoons mayonnaise
- 1 cup shredded cheddar cheese
- 6 bacon pieces, each half-inch thick
- 6 hamburger buns, cut in half

INSTRUCTIONS:
1. Preheat the broiler in your oven.
2. Combine the lunch meat, eggs, cheese cheese, and onion in a food processor, or run them through a grinder until they are finely chopped and combined. Mix in enough mayonnaise to keep it all together once everything has been minced and combined. Spoon equal quantities of the mixture onto the loose buns and top each with two slices of bacon to make a burger sandwich.
3. Broil for 5 to 8 minutes, or until the bacon is crisp, a few inches away from the heat source. Keep an eye on the burgers to make sure they don't burn.

PAD THAI WITH SPAM

INGREDIENTS:
- SPAM Classic (12 ounces), chopped into 1-inch cubes
- 1/2 cup chicken broth
- 1/4 cup creamy peanut butter
- 1/2 cup chicken broth
- 3 and a half teaspoons of soy sauce
- peppercorns freshly ground to your preference

- 1 package (10 ounces) of uncooked udon ramen noodles
- 1 green onion, finely chopped

INSTRUCTIONS:
1. Cook and stir SPAM Classic in a pan over medium heat for 10 minutes, or until it is lightly toasted on both sides. Set aside on a plate lined with paper towels to allow the excess liquid to drain.
2. In a small saucepan over low heat, combine the chicken broth, peanut butter, and soy sauce; simmer, constantly stirring, until a smooth peanut sauce is formed. Serve immediately. Pepper should be added to the peanut sauce.
3. Bring a saucepan of salted water to a boil, then cook the udon noodles for approximately 10 minutes, or until they are soft. Drain the liquid and return it to the saucepan over low heat.
4. Stir the peanut sauce and SPAM Classic into the noodles until the noodles are well covered; transfer to a serving platter and garnish with chopped green onion, if you like.

MINI SPAM SANDWICHES

INGREDIENTS:
- 10 pieces of white bread that have been gently toasted
- 1/2 cup creamy salad dressing, for example, mayonnaise Miracle Whip (also known as Miracle Cream), is a product that can transform any liquid into a miracle whip.
- 1/4-inch-thick slices of Spam from a single 12-ounce container
- 10 pieces of Cheddar cheese, sliced
- 10 thin pineapple slices (about)

INSTRUCTIONS:
1. Each piece of bread should have a thin coating of salad dressing spread on one side alone. Five of the bread pieces should have two slices of Spam sandwiched between them. They should be able to cover the slices completely. Place two slices of cheese on top of each layer of Spam, overlapping them, so they cover the whole piece of bread. Place pineapple slices on top of the cheese,

slicing them into squares to fit between the sandwiches. Place the remaining parts of the bread on top of the salad, with the salad dressing on the inside of each slice. If preferred, trim the crusts of the sandwiches and cut each sandwich into four equal squares.

THE END

Printed in Great Britain
by Amazon